About the author

Allan Goodbrand is an international businessman, seasoned traveller, amateur writer, lover of good food and wine, and father of three grown-up children of whom he is immensely proud. He has a keen interest in the many idiosyncrasies and features of the English language that make it so different from other languages of the world, including idiomatic sayings which seem to be a property almost unique to English.

Know Your Onions
A light-hearted look at popular idioms and sayings

Allan Goodbrand

Book Guild Publishing

First published in Great Britain in 2015 by
The Book Guild Ltd
9 Priory Business Park
Wistow Road, Kibworth
Leics, LE8 0RX
Tel: 0800 999 2982
Email: info@bookguild.co.uk

ISBN 978 1 910508 53 4

MIX
Paper from
responsible sources
FSC® C013056

CONTENTS

Part 2: Of Nautical Origin

Part 3: As Drunk as a Lord

Part 4: Where Did That Come From?

Part 5: Obvious? Perhaps Not

Part 6: Often Mispronounced

Introduction

This book is a light-hearted look at idioms, similes, and other expressions and sayings. An idiom is defined as: *a combination of words that has a figurative meaning – separate from its literal meaning – owing to its common usage*; a useful definition which reminds us that the 'figurative' meaning may be quite different from the literal meaning. Take 'It's raining cats and dogs' – no one in their right mind expects household pets to start falling from the sky and yet we readily use this figurative phrase in the event of a heavy downpour.

Similes are sayings where one thing is compared to another with the aim of elaborating the point being made, for example 'As drunk as a Lord'. This cannot be taken literally to mean that all Lords are drunk (despite what you might think), nor indeed that all drunks are Lords, so there is a figurative aspect to this type of saying too.

It is said that there are more than 10,000 known expressions of this kind in the English language; that's a staggering number. If you were to write down as many as you could think of in a few minutes, without referring to a book such as this, I'll bet you wouldn't get to more than fifty or so, at least not without some serious thinking.

Collected here are those that sparked my interest more than others. I expect that you already know the origin and meaning of some of them, but I am also sure there are more than a few where you do not. My aim is to entertain you as I explain, as best I can, the derivation of these phrases that in many cases have survived for centuries, and that add so much colour to our wonderful language.

PART 1
Of American Origin

It has been said that Britain and America are two nations divided by a common language. As one who has lived and travelled extensively throughout the United States, I can say there have been many occasions when that division has been apparent. Misunderstanding can often result, which is sometimes humorous, sometimes not. One example is 'bonnets' and 'boots'. In the UK, apart from the obvious reference to items of clothing, these also refer to parts of a car, the bonnet being the cover that gives access to the engine and the boot being the storage compartment at the rear. I explain this for the benefit of any American readers; I realise of course that British readers will know this already. But in the United States, the bonnet of a car is called the 'hood' and the boot is called the 'trunk'. The words bonnet and boot are reserved by Americans only for items of headgear and footwear. Imagine the puzzlement and amusement when an ex-patriot Brit looking to buy a car in his new American hometown asks the salesman if he can raise the bonnet and look in the boot!

What follows is a selection of sayings that have their origins firmly across the Atlantic. You may be as surprised as I was to see just how many very common ones have their roots in the United States.

A Ballpark Figure
[an estimate, an approximation]

I expect everyone knows of this saying as it is widely used on both sides of the Atlantic to mean an estimate, or perhaps a 'guestimate'. However, it is intended to have been considered, so is not just a wild guess.

The origin is clearly American, coming from the game of baseball which is played in a 'ballpark'. Unless the hitter is unerringly accurate, which is unusual, baseballs are hit in all sorts of directions, resulting in them landing pretty much anywhere in the ballpark. So the saying means anywhere within the boundaries of the ballpark, or within reasonable limits. *A Ballpark Figure* is an estimated amount.

'For goodness' sake man, I know you haven't had time to calculate it precisely. Just give me *a ballpark figure* of how much the repair will cost.'

A Dime a Dozen
[common, plentiful and readily available]
This has a very obvious meaning and is similar to the English expression 'Two a penny'. Note that I have not defined it as meaning 'cheap' or 'inexpensive' although that might be implied. The real intent is that whatever item or feature is being described is in such plentiful supply that it will not be difficult to acquire many of them. As most people will know, a dime is a ten-cent coin or one-tenth of a dollar.

'Don't waste your time looking in the hotel shop at those trinkets my dear. They'll be *a dime a dozen* down at the local market.'

Behind the Eight Ball
[a tight spot, a tricky situation with no apparent escape route]

There is dispute as to the genuine origin of this saying. The obvious one is a game of eight ball pool, in which the eight ball is the last one that must be played. A ball can be put in an impossible position by getting it to come to rest *Behind the Eight Ball,* thereby putting one's opponent at a distinct disadvantage. However, various sources tell us that the first recorded usage is before eight ball pool was widely played and that it must therefore come from an earlier version of the game which was played with different rules.

Either way, the origin is almost certainly American and from the game of pool. It has become used to describe a generally unfavourable or disadvantaged position, or a troublesome situation.

Between a Rock and a Hard Place
[having to select between two equally bad options]

This is often likened to the saying 'Between the devil and the deep blue sea' and does indeed have the same meaning. Not much of a choice I suppose: would you rather go the devil, or be committed to the deep? Well, neither frankly but that's the point. In this situation one doesn't have the luxury of refusing to choose; it has to be one or the other unpalatable option.

The expression is said to come from mine workers in Arizona in the early 1900s who, having asked their employers for better conditions and been refused, were deported from the United States. The 'rock' was the rock face in the mine and the 'hard place' was unemployment and deportation. Pretty nasty stuff all round given that the general working conditions for miners in those days must have been harsh to say the least.

Blue Chip Company
[of reputable standing, reliable, high value]

Blue chip companies are those of the highest creditworthiness, financial reputation and stability. They will be the most well-known organisations, often the top 100 or so that are included in internationally quoted stock market indexes like the FTSE or the Dow Jones. Their shares are often less volatile than those of lesser firms and are therefore favoured by large institutional investors.

That's all very well, but why 'blue chip'? It comes from the days when poker was gaining popularity as a game across America and organised games, especially those run by casinos, used chips rather than cash to place bets. The blue chips had the highest value and hence the term *Blue Chip Company* was coined to mean of high value.

Boil the Ocean
[to overcomplicate where a simple solution will do]
Most often heard stated in the negative by which I mean it is usual to say, 'Let's not try to boil the ocean,' this is another example of the wonderful way Americans have with words and their uses. Just imagine how impossibly difficult it would be to bring even a small ocean up to boiling point. It is clearly one of those sayings where extreme exaggeration is used to make the point and is one of my all-time favourites.

Bury the Hatchet
*[to settle an argument or disagreement, to cease fighting
and agree to peace]*

This, as might be expected, is of American origin and further it
genuinely originates from Native American tribes. The hatchet
was without doubt a weapon used by these peoples and figu-
ratively to *Bury the Hatchet* clearly means to cease fighting.
But it is said that tribal chiefs literally buried hatchets in the
ground ceremonially, when reaching a peaceful agreement
with an adversary.

Bust One's Chops
[to nag incessantly]
This is a great example of American use of the English language.
The meaning of the word 'bust' here is the same as when used
in 'bust your buns', which means to work hard on something
or to go the extra mile to make sure it is completed on time.
('Buns', incidentally, are one's buttocks, so what is actually
being said is 'bust your ass'.) 'Chops' refers to the jaw or cheeks
– remember those enormous triangular sideburns men grew
in the 1970s, weren't they called 'mutton chops'? Anyway, to
Bust One's Chops is to criticise or nag persistently to the point
of annoyance.

'For God's sake will you stop *busting my chops* about cleaning out the
garage! I'll do it on Saturday.'

Class Action
[a lawsuit involving a group of people]

A *Class Action* is not the same as a 'class act', in other words it does not mean an action that is classy or superior. *Class Action* is a legal term used widely in the United States to describe a law suit, usually brought against a corporation or large organisation, by a group of people (the class) who agree to being 'classed' as a single entity in the legal process, and to being treated as one body rather than separate individuals.

Class action law suits can be a very effective way of ensuring that large powerful bodies (companies or others) cannot get away with skulduggery or underhand activity simply because it would be too costly for any one person to take them on. It might not be cost effective for lawyers to represent a single person in such a case, but if a number of people have all been affected by the same event or activity it might well be practical to bring a class action lawsuit against whoever is responsible. Any settlement achieved is shared by the members of the class.

There are many examples of 'Joe Public' vs. large corporations that demonstrate the power of class actions – one such was popularised in the excellent film *Erin Brockovich* [Universal Pictures, 2000] based on a true story about a public utility company that had contaminated land by illegally dumping toxic waste.

Chew the Fat
[to chat, to make small talk, to kill time chatting]

This might derive from sailors who, centuries ago, chewed salted fat for nourishment, or possibly from Native Americans who chewed animal skins when they were not hunting or were just passing time.

It has come to mean not only chatting idly with no particular purpose, but also just passing the time idly. It may also refer to how one's jaw appears to be chewing when talking, if viewed from out of earshot for example. This is similar to (but not exactly the same as) 'shooting the breeze'.

'Take no notice of Bill and Fred, they're not doing anything important. They're just *chewing the fat*.'

Close But No Cigar
[to come second best, to fall short of the target by a narrow margin and receive nothing in return]

Almost certainly this originates in the United States and is likely to relate to the practice in days gone by of funfairs giving cigars as prizes at various stalls, such as shooting or archery. Such a thing would surely be frowned upon nowadays. Contestants narrowly missing the bulls-eye might be *Close But No Cigar*.

I like to think of this as coming from the American military where, at the end of successful missions, a box of cigars is handed around and each participant lights up a celebratory smoke, but I have found no evidence of this origin.

Cold Turkey
[to give up something immediately, without weaning off gradually]

This has become synonymous with drug addiction and is used to describe either the process of immediate withdrawal from whatever dependency is in question, or the unpleasant effects experienced by someone going through this process.

The original meaning and usage of *Cold Turkey* is more likely to derive from 'talking turkey' or speaking blatantly honestly about a subject. Its association with drug addiction is a twentieth-century development, the linkage being that the addict takes the abrupt, blatant approach. It has nothing whatever to do with having to endure seemingly endless meals of cold turkey after Christmas, or in America after Thanksgiving – at least I can find no evidence of this.

Cut to the Chase
[to get to the heart of the matter]

This is believed to have originated from Hollywood in the era of silent films, where visual action was all the more important as there was no dialogue, and when many such movies had a chase scene which was often the most exciting part of the plot. Hence to *Cut to the Chase* was to dispense with less important pieces of the plot and get to the core of the action.

This expression is used these days to urge someone to deal with the priorities or, to put it another way, to Stop Beating Around the Bush.

Down to the Wire
[at the last moment]

This saying comes from horseracing in the USA, where the finishing line is called the wire (or was in years gone by). Perhaps this was because a wire was used to draw a line across the racecourse. When two or more horses had a chance of winning the race right up to the end, and the race was only decided at the last moment, it was described as being *Down to the Wire*.

The saying is also used to mean a tense situation, as might be the case if you had bet a lot of money on one or other of these horses.

Looking at the tyres on a car I saw parked at the supermarket recently, I noticed they were 'down to the wires' and looked jolly dangerous, although this has no connection whatever with this saying.

'Both teams played their hearts out all the way and the match was down to the wire,' said the radio commentator.

Jump on the Bandwagon
[join a popular movement]

Travelling fairs and circuses were a popular form of entertainment before the days of cinema and television. In order to advertise their arrival in a location, the travelling show would parade their more interesting wagons through the town and one of these would have the band playing on it as they went. People would follow this musical cart and might even get on board themselves, perhaps sitting on the rear so that they could stay with the music and enjoy the festive atmosphere of the arriving circus by *Jumping on the Bandwagon*. Like so many of these phrases, its meaning today is more general and is used to describe the act of following or joining a popular movement.

Jump the Gun
[to start something without completing the necessary preparations]

There is a perfectly simple and obvious origin to this one – quite simply to start the race (albeit momentarily) before the starting gun has actually fired. It is said that contestants have been known to try to do this without it being too noticeable – and years ago, before the days of slow-motion cameras and electronic timing systems, it was possible to do so without penalty and thereby gain an unfair advantage.

The saying is used today in any situation where to start something without being fully prepared is to *Jump the Gun.*

Although he was not advocating starting before the pistol fired, the highly successful British sprinter Linford Christie used to say, 'Go on the B of Bang,' meaning one should be as close to *jumping the gun* as possible without actually breaking the rules!

Kicked Into Touch
[to break off an activity, to stop or to postpone proceedings]

Clearly, the ball being kicked over the touch line or 'into touch' in various sports results in a temporary suspension of the game while the ball is returned to play, and the origin of the saying is just this. It has become adopted in other walks of life than sport, however, and is widely used in the United States in business and generally, where a project or activity has been halted either temporarily or, more often, permanently.

'This fellow is worth a second interview, Vice President, but the others have been *kicked into touch.*'

Know Your Onions
[to be expert in some subject or discipline]

You might be surprised, as I was, to learn that this is of American origin although, once again, there are a number of proposed derivations and disputes as to which is true.

In the mid-1800s a man called Onions supplied schools with teaching-aid counters that mimicked coins so that children could learn about coinage and counting, and hence would *Know their Onions.*

However, reference dictionaries state that the origin of this saying is unknown, and I for one believe them. I suspect it is another one of those phrases that perhaps came into usage many years ago when ranching and farming were widespread, and the knowledge that went with growing crops and vegetables was so important that a person who *knew his onions* was a knowledgeable person indeed.

Mission Creep
[expansion of a project beyond its original scope]

I love the Americans' ability to coin terms and phrases such as these. It seems that new ones come into usage frequently and this is definitely a twentieth-century addition. First used to describe a military operation that had gone way beyond its original intentions in terms of timescale and activity, there are now many examples of non-military use. The term is often heard in business and commercial management where a project has expanded to include more than was initially intended, or more likely to have gone way over budget in cost and/or timescale.

It is not (as one person I consulted, thought) a term used to describe the shifty, nasty person on the mission that no one likes.

Motherhood and Apple Pie
[basic principles – traditional values of American home life]

Americans will say, 'That's like *Motherhood and Apple Pie*,' meaning that something is as basic and obvious as it could possibly be. In fact, the saying derives from the Second World War when US soldiers stationed in Europe and beyond were asked what they missed most from home and they replied, 'Mom and Apple Pie.' So the saying came into use as a euphemism for the sentimental values that personify perfect or ideal American home life. It has been adopted to mean anything which is plain and simple.

Not Playing With a Full Deck
[not clever – lacking in intellect]

This is a put-down that I have often heard and is widely used in America. There are a number of other examples with very similar meaning such as 'not the sharpest tool in the box' which has a certain clarity to it; 'the lights are on but no one is home,' which is a little more obscure; and, one I really like, 'one sandwich short of a picnic', which makes me smile.

Although some card games are specifically designed to be played with fewer than the full deck of cards, most require all cards to be in play for the game to work, so *Not Playing With a Full Deck* would indeed not be very clever. But turning up to a picnic with just one sandwich missing would hardly spoil the event, if in fact it would even be noticed. This shows the distinct difference between the literal and figurative meanings of such idiomatic sayings.

On Cloud Nine
[in a state of complete satisfaction or happiness]

There are a number of possible derivations of this saying. Buddhists attempting to reach enlightenment go through ten stages, the ninth being 'cloud nine'. But why then would the saying not be 'on cloud ten'? Another possible origin refers to the American Weather Bureau's classification of clouds, nine being the white fluffy variety that are so much nicer than those nasty grey rainy types. This has an altogether more romantic feel for my liking, but there is evidence of the saying being in use before cloud classification came about.

One source tells us that the number is not important as it has probably changed over the years anyway, beginning perhaps as cloud seven (possibly linked with 'Seventh Heaven') and has simply risen over time to nine. I have to say this sounds quite likely, as it is clear that many sayings change gradually but sometimes significantly over time.

Pushing the Envelope
[to go beyond the design limits, to go outside the safety zone]

I know a good many people who have never understood this phrase, most of them imagining a person shoving a paper envelope along the table or desktop for some bizarre unknown reason.

But in fact it refers to the 'operational envelope' or list of specifications, originally of aircraft, and was possibly used by test pilots when exploring exactly how far they could push a new aeroplane – right to the edge of its design limits, and sometimes beyond, hopefully without catastrophic results.

Now the saying is used to describe any situation where something is being exercised near to or at its intended limits, and although other countries were involved in the development of aircraft, I believe it is of American origin.

Put Your John Hancock on Here
[to add one's signature]

John Hancock (1737–1793) was an American statesman and patriot who rebelled against British rule and in 1776 was instrumental in the American Declaration of Independence. There were at that time 13 separate colonies or states who were the original signatories and Hancock was the governor of one of these states, Massachusetts. As such, he was one of the first to sign the Declaration and his signature is very prominent, giving rise to the saying *Put your John Hancock on Here* when asking someone to sign their name on a document.

For those non-American readers, the American flag has 13 stripes because of these original 13 states, and 50 stars representing the number of states in the Union today.

A British version of this saying is 'put your moniker on here' and there are various proposed origins of this. I prefer the one that derives from Cockney rhyming slang which links *Monica James* (a writer) with *names*, hence 'put your name on here', but other explanations are equally plausible and might well be correct.

Shoot the Breeze
[casually chat, to talk matters of little importance]

Similar to 'chew the fat', although that is more to do with killing time with idle chatter. This seems to indicate more of a relaxed and casual conversation, perhaps with the sun going down and a drink in hand. I cannot find definitive evidence for the origin of this, but I like to think of it deriving from a breeze being a light and easy wind – hence light and easy chatter rather than deep serious debate. I have included it as being of American origin because I have heard it said in the USA many times, but seldom at home or elsewhere.

Sold Down the River
[betrayed, let down]

This originates from the days of the slave trade in the United States, when slaves were bought by traders from northern states and re-sold for a profit to work in southern areas, often going from domestic work to much harder labour and often in far worse conditions. One route for this trade was the Mississippi river hence the term to be *Sold Down the River*. Once again, I am surprised, not by the origin of the saying, but that it has endured over time even though the horrible activities surrounding slavery have long since ceased. The saying is used today to imply any form of betrayal.

Soup to Nuts
[from start to finish, the whole thing]

This is another example of the beautiful simplicity and logic of some American sayings. It just refers to a full dinner with many courses, starting with a soup and ending with a dessert or other dish comprising or including nuts.

I suspect this is fairly recent addition possibly even in the last half century or so.

Take a Rain Check
[to postpone an invitation to another time]

Time was that, if a baseball game were to be rained off, spectators could use their ticket stub to gain admission to the game when it was re-played in better weather, the word 'check' being the American spelling of cheque, implying a promissory note.

This has now come to be used when an invitation must be declined due to other commitments, but would be welcome at another time.

'Can you make it for a drink after work tonight Pete?'

'Sorry, I'm picking the kids up so I'll have to *take a rain check.*'

Take the Fifth
[to remain silent, to refuse to answer a question]

As all American readers will know, but others might not, this arises from the Fifth Amendment to the American Constitution, which states that everyone has the right not to testify against themselves in a court of law if it will incriminate them. It is euphemistically used in any situation where someone has decided to remain silent for whatever reason, often being described as 'pleading the fifth'.

The Dog and Pony Show
[a polished presentation or performance]

This derives quite simply from the days when touring circuses or fairs would use dogs and horses to perform as one of the main attractions or sideshows, the animals being exceptionally well trained to give a practised and enchanting performance.

I have heard this used by sales teams in professional business situations, when perfecting their presentations with the intention of delivering a full *Dog and Pony Show* to prospective clients.

The Whole Nine Yards
[everything, the whole thing]

You might be disappointed to learn that there isn't any clever or meaningful origin to this one. I used to think it related to baseball or American football, but there is no move or score that depends on a distance of nine yards. It turns out that this is another saying that might have been subject to 'inflation' over the years as apparently it began as 'the whole six yards'. That's as may be, but it is certainly in daily usage now, as are others with similar meanings, such as the following.

'The whole shebang'; I am still unsure what a shebang is, having found no definitive answer. 'The whole ball of wax'; I believe this is derived from a lottery system used to allocate plots of land where a ticket with a number is folded and waxed into a ball so that the number cannot be seen before drawing it. 'The whole enchilada'; this at least has a sensible meaning, as lovers of Mexican food will know, in that an enchilada contains just about everything: meat, cheese, beans, the lot. Quite delicious.

Throw the Baby Out With the Bathwater
[to inadvertently throw the good out with the bad]

In fact, this is most often quoted as 'Don't throw the baby out with the bathwater', in order to avoid the mistake of jettisoning the good part of something while ridding oneself of the bad parts. I don't believe the suggested origin, that babies might not have been seen in the dim light and murky bathwater of the Middle Ages, and that there was therefore literally a risk of poor baby being thrown away while tipping the water from the hand-tub, but stranger things have proved to be true.

To Hell in a Hand Basket
[heading for certain disaster]

Sometimes 'going to hell in a handcart'. These sayings are used to describe a situation that is rapidly worsening, or which is heading for certain disaster. Like so many idioms the origin is unclear, but I like to think that there is some connection with the practice of guillotining one's enemies or prisoners, perhaps around the time of the French Revolution. As those unfortunates were executed, their heads were caught in a hand-basket, the souls of the dead almost certainly being thought to be despatched to hell, hence *To Hell in a Hand Basket*. Many other possible derivations are suggested, but none seems any more likely than another to me, and this is the one I prefer.

As for the meaning to imply heading for disaster – I suppose for the poor person being dragged to the guillotine, well, they truly were heading for disaster, weren't they?

PART 2
Of Nautical Origin

It is true that a good many of the most common idioms are genuinely of nautical origin, but it seems that more are thought to have come from seafaring than is actually the case. Quite why this should be is unclear to me. Perhaps the romance of sailing the seven seas has something to do with it or perhaps sailors really did spend a good amount of their time thinking up sayings – I doubt it! Surely their daily lives would have been too full with hard graft and rough conditions to have bothered with such frivolities? Nevertheless, those I have selected here almost certainly have some nautical heritage.

A Loose Cannon
[unpredictable, liable to cause damage]

Imagine the scene: a warship of the seventeenth or eighteenth century, armed on three decks with dozens of heavy cast-iron cannons which, like all weapons of this type, have huge recoil backwards when fired. With the ship swaying at sea these guns, which were on wheels, needed to be firmly secured by a rope such that they could recoil but be stopped from running free. A loose cannon had the potential to roll about the deck in an uncontrolled way, injuring crew and damaging the ship.

These days, rather than a weapon, the term usually describes a person who is thought to be dangerous if not kept in check.

'Watch out for Jones by the way. If you ask me he's *a loose cannon.*'

A Shot Across the Bows
[a warning shot, generally a stern warning]

In the days when sailing ships were used for war it was common naval practice when sighting the enemy to fire a cannon shot in front of the bows of the other craft, to show you were prepared to do battle, or to demonstrate superiority and frighten them into surrender.

This saying is now used in a general sense, in conflict or potentially confrontational situations where a warning 'shot' is fired either literally or metaphorically.

All at Sea
[to be in a state of disarray or chaos]

In the days before modern navigation and communication, any ship on a voyage out of sight of land, or 'at sea', was potentially in danger of being lost. Therefore if your ships were all at sea you simply did not know what might become of them until they were sighted or until they docked again.

To be *All at Sea* has become a way of expressing confusion and disorder.

Batten Down the Hatches
[to prepare for bad weather, to protect against a storm]

Hatches in ships' decks are the doorways giving access to below, for the crew to reach gun decks and lower quarters, and for goods to be stowed. In bad weather, or when preparing for a long voyage, these hatches were covered with planks or tarpaulins held firmly in place by thin strips of wood or battens nailed in place, and so the crew quite literally *Battened Down the Hatches*.

The saying has become a euphemism for preparing for impending trouble of any kind.

By and Large
[all things considered]

This is a combination of two nautical terms. A strong wind behind the ship is referred to as 'large' and when in this orientation the largest sails can be set square-on to the vessel, giving fast downwind travel. 'By' means almost the opposite to sailors, in that it refers to sailing across or towards the wind.

In nautical terms 'by and large' means a ship that, by virtue of its configuration and rig, has the capability to sail either downwind or towards the wind in pretty much any conditions. Thus *By and Large* really means 'under any conditions' but is also used in place of 'all things considered'.

Chock-a-Block
[very tightly packed together, jammed tightly]

Sailing ships used what are called 'block and tackle' hoisting equipment to raise cargo and swing it onto the deck or into holds on the ship. The block is a wooden device with an arrangement of pulleys which allowed heavy weights to be raised by sailors pulling on the ropes. Two or more of these blocks were sometimes put on a single rope system to allow even heavier loads to be lifted. When working this system really hard, the two blocks sometimes moved towards each other and jammed together. At this point they were said to be choked or 'chock-a-block'. So when the ship was being heavily loaded, and when the pulley systems were being worked to their limits, the term would often be heard.

It is said that this term might also refer to the 'chocks' that were used to secure barrels and other containers from rolling or moving in the hold, hence a tightly packed cargo might be

Chock-a-Block.

Of course the term is used in a non-nautical sense these days, often to describe the appalling state of traffic in towns and cities. I particularly like the colloquialisms that have arisen, such as 'chocker' to describe such chaos.

Copper Bottomed
[reliable, genuine]

High-quality saucepans might literally be copper bottomed – made of aluminium or stainless steel but with a bottom made of or covered with copper. Copper is an excellent conductor of heat and gives a very even temperature across the pan. But idiomatically, *Copper Bottomed* is generally used to mean something of reliable quality.

The nautical origin of this comes from wooden ships having sheets of copper (used because of its softness and the ease with which it could be folded and formed around the hull) fixed to their bottoms below the water line to protect against barnacles and other sea creatures known to cause damage to untreated wooden hulls.

The best ships, and many of those of the Royal Navy in the late 1700s, were of wooden construction but *Copper Bottomed.*

Cut and Run
[to make a hasty departure]

This probably derives from seafaring when ships wished to leave port hastily or secretly for whatever reason, perhaps under cover of darkness. Taking time to haul up the anchor and set sail might be noticed so, in order to avoid this, the sailors simply cut the anchor rope and put to sea. Perhaps the captain spread the word to the crew, 'Get ready, we're going to cut and run.'

It is possible this was also the action of stealing a ship from port without being noticed.

The saying has another slightly different meaning when used in the context of more modern warfare, when to cut and run can be used to imply a cowardly retreat or a reversal of strategy. In business too, to cut one's losses and get out of an undesirable contract or situation might be described as to *Cut and Run.*

There is a feeling of some sort of sacrifice being associated with the saying – that one is prepared to give something up in order to escape or get out of an awkward situation. Cutting losses certainly has this element to it and I suppose in the original nautical context the sailors were sacrificing their anchor and some ropes, which undoubtedly had a value.

Go by the Board
[to have finished with, to have no further use for]

The origin is almost certainly nautical as the 'board' is the side of a ship. When something has *Gone by the Board* it has been jettisoned or thrown over the side.

'Oh that's **gone by the board**. We've finished with that idea now and are on to the next one.'

Hand Over Fist
[at a good rate of progress]

This probably originates from pulling on a rope that is hauling something heavy, the technique being to pull with one hand (probably the stronger arm) and hold the rope in that position with the other hand by making a fist, returning to pull some more with the first hand again, thereby making good progress *Hand over Fist.*

This saying is used today to mean anything that is developing rapidly or progressing well.

'They're making money *hand over fist* on that coconut shy, vicar.'

High and Dry
[stranded, possibly without hope]

Definitely of sailing origin, 'high' meaning to be out of the water and 'dry' implying that it might have been quite some time since the hull has seen any water. Typically this would have referred to ships that had become beached, and perhaps had little chance of re-floating without an exceptionally high tide.

Know the Ropes
[to be well acquainted with how to perform a task or tasks]

I think everyone knows this one, but just in case you don't, here is my take on it. The rigging of a sailing ship relies on a vast number of ropes to tether and move sails and other pieces of the rig, and seamen had to know what each of these ropes was for. This saying is quite logical therefore – it simply means that an experienced sailor was one who *Knew the Ropes*. It also gives rise to the saying 'show you the ropes', where a trainee would be put alongside an older hand to learn the purpose of each rope.

Money For Old Rope
[to get paid for something thought to be worthless]

It is said that hangmen used to sell the rope they had used to make the noose that hanged an unfortunate individual con-demned to that fate, and that people would pay good money for such as a souvenir of the event. Pretty macabre if you ask me! If true, this does not belong in the nautical origin section.

But I think a more likely source is that of old worn-out hemp ropes being sold for the fibres to be unpicked and used as 'oakum' – a kind of grouting which was mixed with tar and stuffed into the gaps between planks in wooden ships to seal them watertight, the transaction being literally *Money For Old Rope*.

It is also possible that sailors would take the long ropes used on ships when they were past their useful life and would no longer take the loads required on board, and cut them into shorter lengths to sell on shore for other less-demanding purposes.

The saying is used today to describe getting paid for something that is considered of no value, or is used in a derogatory way to indicate that someone is getting cash for doing very little.

'What's that? Barnes has been made up to manager and got a pay rise? But he's useless. That's *money for old rope*, I tell you.'

Push the Boat Out
[a generous or extravagant gesture]

Again, this has a very logical nautical meaning. Boats that had become beached (see *High and Dry*) had to be pushed back into the water. If the vessel was large and heavy, this was too difficult a task for one man or even a small crew to do on their own. So others would help, and this act of generosity was known as helping to *Push the Boat Out*.

Now the term is used to mean any generous act, or perhaps spending more than is normal on an item or on a treat for oneself or others.

Shake a Leg
[get out of bed]

This is another one that many will know already. Apparently, sailors in their bunks were woken by the command *Shake a Leg* (or perhaps show a leg) meaning they should stick one of their legs out from under the covers to indicate that they were awake and their willingness to get out of bed in the next few moments. There are other possible origins, including that of women sometimes being allowed to travel on voyages and showing their legs from under the covers so that they did not have to get up with the crew, but I prefer the first definition.

'Come on Smith, **shake a leg** you lazy b ...!'

Shipshape and Bristol Fashion
[*in excellent order, well turned out, spick and span*]

Bristol is a port that has prospered due to seafaring. It had an inner harbour dating back many years and, although not used today, it had the benefit that ships could sail right into the centre of the city and dock alongside the buildings of the main shipping companies. This inner harbour was shallow and vessels might list to one side or the other when berthing, so it was necessary to have everything on board tied down and stowed neatly to stop loose items rolling about the ship. So the term *Shipshape and Bristol Fashion* is thought to derive from this and has come to mean a neat and tidy state of affairs, in every sense of the words.

Shiver My Timbers
[*astonishment, surprise*]

Shiver My Timbers (or shiver *me* timbers if you are speaking with a Long John Silver accent) is a gasp of surprise if said by a sailor. 'Shiver' means to break or shatter, and was a common term due to ships' timbers regularly being shattered by cannon fire, a frightening experience I'm sure. In rough seas the main timbers of a ship would creak and groan and might shiver or break in extreme conditions.

So the term *Shiver My Timbers* means something like, 'Oh my God – what the devil is happening?' or perhaps much more colourful language as was undoubtedly used by sailors of the day. The saying can also mean fear and awe, and in the sixteenth and seventeenth centuries was often related to quite horrific circumstances.

Slush Fund
[money used to pay bribes]

Slush to you and me probably means melting snow, but it was also the word for the fatty liquid that is yielded when boiling meat. Pork and beef were prepared in this way when at sea and, although it is a ghastly sludge, slush had its uses and was collected by cooks who would sell it when they reached the next port. The money raised was referred to as the 'slush fund' and there is record of this being put to good use to provide for the crew.

A *Slush Fund* for bribes or other underhand payments, especially in a political context, is a modern usage.

Swinging the Lead
[laziness, shirking work without good reason]

Although there is some dispute about the origin of this saying, it is most likely a reference to the days when sailing ships would throw ropes with lead weights attached to them over the side to determine the depth of water around the vessel. When the weight no longer pulled the rope down, it had reached the bottom, and the depth could be read by counting marks on the rope. Presumably a sailor who couldn't be bothered to throw the ropes and haul them back up again properly would simply swing the rope around, to give the impression that he was hard at work on this task, whereas in fact he was just *Swinging the Lead.*

It might also be that the task of doing this depth measuring was considered by the crew to be much easier than many of the more strenuous jobs on board, and so that is how the saying arose.

'Lucky old Johnson, he's been taken off the sails today and is just *swinging the lead.*'

The Bitter End
[at the limit of one's ability or capacity]

This does not, as you might think, mean that the end has a bitter taste (metaphorically speaking) although it might well have. A 'bitt' is a wooden pillar on the deck of a ship which ropes are fastened to or wound around. The word 'bitter' might refer to the action of wrapping a rope around a bitt, or possibly to the sailor carrying out this task.

When feeding rope out, when there is no more rope to go, you will have come to *The Bitter End.*

The Cut of Your Jib
[one's appearance and presence]

The 'jib' is a triangular sail spanning the fore mast and the boom at the front of a ship. As different countries had different-shaped jibs, the nationality of a vessel could be known from this, and hence whether they were friend or foe. Enemy ships might well draw the comment, 'I don't like the cut of her jib.'

Now this expression is used to describe anything one doesn't like the look of. It is often applied to a person and perhaps to the way they are dressed or present themselves.

'I don't like *the cut of your jib* young man,' boomed the admiral to the new recruit.

Three Sheets to the Wind
[incapably drunk]

Sailors are often drinkers it seems, so perhaps it is not surprising that some of our sayings about drunkenness hail from seafaring.

Sheets in this sense are not, as you might expect, sails. They are the ropes that tie the bottom corners of sails in place. Any of these sheets being loose will cause the sail to blow about – three sheets being loose is enough to cause the sail and the ship to sway uncontrollably like a drunken sailor, and hence be *Three Sheets to the Wind.*

Tide (Me) Over
[to make what you have last until further stock arrives]

This refers literally to a situation in which there is no wind, so it is necessary to allow the ship to be carried by the tide until the wind rises again, hence to *Tide Over.* The meaning has changed over the years, being used today more generally to imply getting through a lean patch until better times return.

'I just need a small amount to **tide me over**, Daddy, until my next student loan payment arrives.'

PART 3
As Drunk as a Lord

Similes are sayings where a comparison is used to illustrate or elaborate the point being made, and there are many of them. To simply say someone is drunk might not go far enough, but to say that he or she is 'as drunk as a Lord' – well, that makes it absolutely clear that in your opinion they are completely plastered, and no more need be said.

Here are a few of the more common and frequently heard examples.

As Bald as a Coot
[*completely bald, hairless*]

To fully understand this you need to know that a coot is a water bird with a large white spot on the front of its otherwise black head. This gives the appearance of a receding hairline and is most probably the origin of the saying. It might also be that 'piebald', a term used to describe animals with spotted coats or white patches, has over time become shortened to 'bald' and that originally the saying was 'as piebald as a coot', although this is less likely and does not of course imply hairlessness.

Another alternative is that when coots raise their heads from underwater, the wetness of their black feathers makes them appear silky and shiny, a sort of bald-looking appearance. Whichever is correct, to be *As Bald as a Coot* is to be pretty much without any hair on one's head at all.

As Blind as a Bat
[*very poorly sighted, clumsy and frequently bumping into things*]

Bats are not really blind; they have eyesight and can see during the day but it is not their strongest sense by a long way. As we all know, their sonar system uses sounds emitted and received back by highly sensitive hearing, almost uniquely among animals, and this serves as highly accurate 'vision' at night, when bats prefer to come out and feed on airborne insects and the like.

To say someone is *As Blind as a Bat* might be a suggestion that they have lost their sight, but it is also used in a more jocular way when a person is clumsy or is seen to bump into items of furniture, for example, as if they could not see very well.

As Bold as Brass
[over-confident, arrogant]

To be bold is to be self-assured and confident, or even brave, and *As Bold as Brass* is to be brimming with self-confidence, perhaps displaying a little too much of it or with little regard for the feelings of others.

That's all very well, but why 'brass'? Research shows that this might be derived from a Mr Brass Crosby who, as Mayor of London in the 1770s, disagreed strongly with parliament that their debates should be private, and supported the printing of these records for public circulation. His bold stance on this issue gave rise to the saying.

It is also true that the word 'brassy' was used centuries ago to describe arrogant confidence or shamelessness, and this could therefore have something to do with the origin.

'In he marched, **as bold as brass**, and demanded we turn the volume down! Well, what a cheek.'

As Bright as a Button
[intelligent, fast thinking, quick witted]

Notice that this saying does not mean that something is shiny – brightness definitely refers here to being bright and brainy. The comparison to a button is a likeness to the shininess of military buttons, which were always polished to sparkling, to amplify that the person in question truly is very smart indeed.

As Clean as a Whistle
[*spotlessly clean*]

Why should a whistle be clean, so clean that it is used in this simile? In the days of steam trains, locomotives had steam whistles which made a very loud sound. Any dirt or grime inside the whistle might affect its tone or volume, so it had to be clean to perform correctly. Also, the action of blowing steam through it at high pressure would have the effect of cleaning it, and I believe this to be the origin of this simile.

It might of course be referring to the tone of the whistle in a similar way to the saying 'as clear as a bell', but I think it is more to do with the cleansing effect of blowing a whistle, whether with steam or by mouth.

As Clear as a Bell
[*clearly understood*]

Sometimes this is expressed as 'as sound as a bell', but the meaning is the same. Bells are cast from metal and are intended to be rung; in other words they are produced for their quality of making sounds. Bells to be used musically (as in church bells – although some might say this is not music) must have a single and clear tone without what are called overtones or harmonics that destroy the single clear note. So one definition of *As Clear as a Bell* can be that a good bell has a clear tone. There is more to this, however: a bell that is cast with an imperfection or one that cracks when cooling down from the casting process will not ring clearly. So only a good bell has a clear tone.

But the definition relates to clarity of understanding, not tonal or musical quality. Bells have been used since their very beginning as warning or signalling devices – a fire bell, for example. Before electric bells and other signals, the bell in a church tower or other building might be rung to warn of some approaching attack or impending danger and hence the message would be received and understood *As Clear as a Bell*.

As Daft as a Brush
[silly, laughable, behaving in a foolish manner]

There are references that suggest this comes from the time when small boys were sent up or down chimneys in order to sweep out the soot, and that because they often banged their heads, sometimes injuring themselves quite badly, they were knocked senseless and were therefore *As Daft as a Brush*. That sounds a little fanciful to me, so although I know for sure that boys were used in this awful way, I doubt that it is the origin of the saying.

   I think it more likely that the reference is to brushes being soft, perhaps the tail of a fox which is called a brush, and to the old English term of being 'soft in the head' meaning quite literally that the brain has gone pulpy, rendering the person mindlessly foolish.

As Drunk as a Skunk
[intoxicated, perhaps to excess]

I was certain this came about purely because 'skunk' rhymes with 'drunk' and thereby makes a neat little saying, albeit not a particularly logical one. There might also be something in the suggestion that the smell of a skunk is being likened to the smell of alcohol, although I think this is a fairly weak link. If a skunk is considered to be not a very nice animal, the term could be intended to be derogatory in that the person in question is not very nice when they are *As Drunk as a Skunk.*

I have since heard that the saying might originate from skunks eating fermenting berries and becoming intoxicated by the alcohol so produced, and then acting in a drunken manner. I like the idea of this, but why only skunks and not any other animals? Also, I don't recall seeing any of this on the countless nature programmes on television these days, so I am not so sure.

Either way, to be *As Drunk as a Skunk* is to be completely sloshed.

As Dry as a Bone
[very dry, arid]

Another very simple and obvious definition. Most of us only see bones either in a butcher's shop or in some other context of food. But when bones are found while digging in the garden or exploring a piece of land, they have usually been there for some time and are the remains of an animal that is long since dead. Unlike the bones in the cut of meat for Sunday roast, those in the ground have given up all of their marrow and moisture and are all but completely dry. Hence the term *As Dry as a Bone*, or bone dry.

As Fit as a Butcher's Dog
[in good health, very fit or perhaps well fed]

This is pretty clear; it simply means that a butcher's dog has a plentiful supply of fresh bones and meat, albeit the parts of meat that the butcher can't sell to his customers, and is therefore well fed. It does not necessarily mean that the dog is in good shape physically and it is of course possible that a butcher's dog might become fat and lazy. Generally, the saying is used today to describe someone who is in good health.

It is not linked to the use of the term 'fit' when describing a member of the opposite sex who is attractive and sexually alluring, as is common with men and women eyeing up a potentially suitable partner, whether for the evening or the rest of their lives.

As Fit as a Fiddle
[in excellent health, in fine form]

There does not appear to be a clear origin of this saying. Some references point to 'fit' meaning suitable, while others suggest that musical instruments like violins or fiddles had to be kept in good condition in order to play well.

I wonder if this is more to do with the fiddler himself than the fiddle. There is a certain liveliness and vivacity to fiddle playing, especially in pubs and the sort of places fiddlers might entertain. The brio and energy of a jig played on a fiddle might well give rise to the saying *As Fit as a Fiddle* in my view.

As Happy as a Sand Boy
[happy, completely satisfied, relaxed]

A sand boy was someone who collected and delivered sand to inns and other establishments to spread on the floor as a means of soaking up spilled ale and other liquids, in the same way that sawdust was sometimes used. They were not necessarily boys and might well have been grown men, the term 'boy' meaning that this was a fairly lowly occupation. But why would they be happy in this task? I am sure they were paid at least partly in cash for the sand, otherwise they would not have been able to continue in business, but they were apparently also paid partly (or perhaps sometimes only) in beer. Imagine delivering to a dozen or more hostelries and having a pint in each. It would not be long before the effects were felt and this would be where the happiness comes in.

It might be just as correct to describe them as being tipsy or even drunk, but the saying *As Happy as a Sand Boy* has stuck and is still heard widely today.

'Is young Tom all right do you think?'
'Yes, no problem with him, he's *as happy as a sand boy.*'

As High as a Kite
[intoxicated, high on drugs]

Toy kites have been flown for fun for many years, but I think this saying is actually referring to a type of falcon called a red kite. These birds of prey soar quite high above the ground and I can well image people in days gone by marvelling at the sight of them. Originally, then, to be *As High as a Kite* might have referred to something flying high in the air.

Today's usage is different. The word 'high' is now used to mean under the influence of drugs or possibly alcohol, and modern use of the saying usually means someone is high on drugs.

As Mad as a March Hare
[completely bonkers]

This comes literally from the observation of hares acting in an apparently daft manner in the month of March, probably because this is the breeding season for hares (in Europe), when the males engage in energetic activities such as jumping up on their hind legs and seeming to 'box' with each other. This has been recorded in literature since at least the 1500s and of course the 'March Hare' appears as a character in Lewis Carroll's works. It is probably also linked with the saying 'a hare-brain scheme' (see Part 6), again referring to madness.

The saying is used today to describe someone who has taken leave of their senses and is therefore *As Mad as a March Hare.*

As Mad as a Hatter
[mad, crazy]

A simple enough definition and origin for this one. Mercury is a metallic element that was sometimes the fun stuff in school chemistry classes. Commonly known as quicksilver, it is liquid at room temperature and when poured out runs all over the desk, separating into globules while glistening like liquid silver. It has many uses, for example in thermometers and fluorescent lighting, but it was also once used in hat making. Felt soaked in mercury compounds produced a finer finish and superior grade material compared to others and was therefore used to make the finest hats. Unfortunately, like many heavy metals, mercury is highly toxic and has a detrimental effect on human mental faculty, resulting in personality changes and mood swings at the least and, with continued exposure, eventually madness.

Although there is some dispute that this is the actual origin, I think the evidence is too strong for it not to be the case. I suspect there were a number of people who worked as hatters who had regrettably gone bonkers, thus giving rise to the saying. Another of Lewis Carroll's fictional characters is based on this idea.

As Old as the Hills
[very old, long ago]

I believe this might have a biblical origin. If so, it has survived very well as it is used today in the same form and with the same meaning. There is nothing clever or hidden – in referring to humans or to things that are man-made, As Old as the Hills literally refers to the land having been here well before us and therefore very much older in relative terms.

When we say this now, we don't of course mean literally as old as the creation of the Earth, but we are expressing the idea that something or someone has been around for a very long time.

As Right as Ninepence

[perfectly well, on top form, everything all right and as expected]

There are quite a few 'as right as ...' similes. I've included just two here and neither seems to make much sense. There has been much evolution of these phrases with many different words involved. For example 'as right as a trivet' (a pot or kettle stand) was popular at some time in the past. The only logic in this could be that the kettle stands safe and upright on the stable trivet, whereas it might fall into the fire otherwise.

Although a couple of hundred years ago, when ale was a penny a pint, it would have been nice to have ninepence of spare change in your pocket, there is really no reason for this not being ten pence or a shilling (if any readers are old enough to remember what a shilling was). But what if 'ninepence' is actually a mispronunciation of 'nine pins', the game of skittles where the pins are set up in a neat square before rolling heavy balls at them? There seems to be a theme here about things being upright or square, or safe and firm, and perhaps this is the correct origin and meaning of *As Right as Ninepence*.

As Right as Rain

[perfectly well, on top form, everything all right and as expected]

Apart from rain falling in straight lines (but not always) and thereby linking with the previous definition, this makes no real sense. I suppose that rain might have been accepted as the normal weather in certain parts of the country and therefore to be *As Right as Rain* was for everything to be normal and as expected. Hmm, maybe!

As Scarce as Hens' Teeth
[rarely occurring, perhaps not existing at all]

Clearly, hens do not have teeth. They would never be able to fit them into their beaks anyway. Seriously, to be as scarce as something that doesn't exist because it is actually an impossibility – that's very rare indeed. There are other similar sayings to make the point that something is so rare as to not really exist. 'As rare as rocking horse s**t' is one that comes to mind; if you find some of that, then there is something very strange going on.

As Sober as a Judge
[a serious disposition]

I have seen definitions of this suggesting that the meaning is connected with sobriety, or with not being drunk when others around you are intoxicated. That might be a useful picture to have in your mind when looking for the meaning here, but I think a more correct description is that of being serious or grave in nature.

Judges always appear to be the sombre, unemotional presence in the court room, occasionally even grim. They never laugh when something funny is said and rigidly stick to procedure, necessarily so it has to be said. Imagine the situation when sentencing a convict – seriousness is certainly what would be expected, especially in cases where capital punishment penalties were being pronounced.

So, to be *As Sober as a Judge* I believe means to be serious and stern.

As Thick as Thieves
[closest friends, confidants]

This does not of course mean that all thieves are thick in the not-very-clever sense of the word. Thick here means to be tightly bound in friendship or comradeship, and it was presumably thought that camaraderie between thieves was unusually strong, so this simile came about.

This is used today to describe any group of people, two or more, who are not themselves thieves, but who are either very friendly or who stick together in any given situation.

'You won't get him to tell you anything about John Smith. They're *as thick as thieves,* those two.'

PART 4
Where Did That Come From?

My interest in idioms and sayings is as much about their origin as it is about explaining their meaning and use. Origins might be entirely factual, as in the 'Acid Test' for example, where acid is actually used to perform an analysis, or they might be based on some physical item, such as 'Cash on the Nail' where the 'nail' is a metal table shaped like a large nail, or they might even have a biblical foundation, as in the instance of a 'Doubting Thomas'.

This section deals with expressions where I am attracted as much by the likely origin as by the saying itself.

A Little Bird Told Me
[from a secret source – unwilling to divulge the source]

There is more than one suggested origin of this phrase. Some say it is biblical in that it refers to 'that which has wings shall tell' in certain passages of the Bible, although I cannot be sure that this is correct source of the saying.

Shakespeare uses the device of a bird bringing secret information to characters in several plays, as a way of communicating a 'secret' which would be difficult to weave into the plot in any other way.

Although there may be some truth in these proposed origins, it is just as likely that the expression has come about when people, not wishing to embarrass the source of some piece of sensitive or confidential information, simply say that *A Little Bird Told Me.*

A Right Two and Eight
[in a mess]

This is very straightforward – it is Cockney rhyming slang for 'a right state'. Interestingly, rhyming slang is often used to 'hide' the real intended meaning by only speaking one word of the phrase that rhymes with the actual meaning. For example, 'Brussels sprout' is rhyming slang for 'boy scout' but it is spoken as only 'Brussels', so hiding the word that actually rhymes. This gives the slang its additional quality of being a secret language.

But in the case we are considering the whole phrase is spoken, and anything that is badly awry can be said to be in *A Right Two and Eight.*

Acid Test

[a reliable test that will give an absolutely certain result]

Gold is what is known as a noble metal, which means it does not easily react with other elements. That is why it doesn't tarnish or rust. But it does react with 'Aqua Regia' (literally Royal Water) a mixture of nitric and hydrochloric acids – in fact, gold will dissolve in this highly corrosive liquid.

Before modern analytical methods were developed, the only certain way to test if a metal was truly gold was to apply the *Acid Test*. This was done by applying a small amount of 'Aqua Fortis' (pure nitric acid) which dissolves all metals other than gold. If a reaction is observed, the metal cannot be pure gold. However, if no reaction is observed then a small amount of Aqua Regia is applied, and if a reaction takes place it is certain that the material is gold.

In the California Gold Rush years (c. 1850s) traders were able to apply this test in the field and thereby determine reliably that prospectors' spoils were indeed gold. The saying is sometimes used to describe the veracity of a person's character, or the validity of a product or service.

Apple of Your Eye

[someone special to you, a dear loved one, a favourite child]

This saying appears in works by Shakespeare but it was not coined by him, as it is also mentioned numerous times in the Bible so has been in use for quite some time. I discovered that in translation from Hebrew it literally means 'little man of the eye' and, as there are various biblical occurrences of the term, I believe the Hebrew meaning to be important in determining its origin. The little man of the eye seems to relate to the tiny reflected image one can see of oneself in the dark central part of the eye of another person. I fancy that this might be a reference to 'being in one's own image' which also has religious significance as God is said to have created man in his own image, in other words to look just like himself.

So I believe that 'apple' is simply a mistranslation and the saying has come into common usage probably through its repeated use in literature over the years. Used today it means that someone is especially cherished or quite possibly is the image of their parent.

At Sixes and Sevens
[confused or in disarray]

This derives from a game of dice called 'hazard' in which a player has to say a number between five and nine and then throw this figure as the total of two dice. As there is a slightly different probability of throwing a total of 6 or 7, due to the different number of combinations that add up to these figures, the saying almost certainly originally meant to foolishly or recklessly risk everything. You might have spotted that this game is in fact the predecessor of 'craps', which was and still is very popular in America. Quite how the meaning became one of confusion is not clear from what I have been able to find.

Another theory offered is that two Trades Guilds or Livery Companies in London in the 1400s could not agree as to which of them had been established before the other and therefore which was sixth in the order of precedence, and which was seventh, a matter that was seemingly extremely important to them. It was apparently settled by the then Lord Mayor, who decided that the two companies would alternate between sixth and seventh place each year and thereby share the ranking.

They were, it was said, constantly *At Sixes and Sevens* with each other, a state of confusion of some sort, I suppose.

At The Drop of a Hat
[immediately, instantly, a signal to go, very eager]

In days gone by, hats were worn as part of normal dress and pretty much everyone wore such headgear every day. Hats are of course functional in protecting from rain and weather, but they are also part of a uniform, for example identifying a policeman or other officer as a member of the service to which he or she belongs. They can be used to signal, being waved for example to make oneself better seen, or thrown in the air in celebration.

I think it is this ability to signal that is important here. I believe that the origin of the saying is simply that a hat was dropped to indicate the start of a contest or some other event, and that the action signified that it was the moment for the contestants to begin.

The saying is often used to mean that someone is a little over eager to start something and that perhaps they should be somewhat more restrained, as in the example below.

'Oh yes, I'm sure he will take up the offer *at the drop of a hat.*'

Bring Home the Bacon
[to earn money for family upkeep, to provide for the household]

It is interesting that bacon crops up more than once in idiomatic sayings – to 'save my bacon' for example, which features later in this section. Bacon did not mean only the part of the pig that we use it to mean today. Years ago 'bacon' was used for any edible cut of meat from any animal, making the meaning more logical in that it referred to any meat brought home to help nourish the family. There is also a linkage with prizes: one story tells of a landowner rewarding the loyalty of a couple who worked on his lands with a side of bacon; another is of bacon or meat being given as a prize for some contest or other, so in both of these cases they quite literally *Brought Home the Bacon.*

The saying has also been linked with boxing or prize-fighting, but I believe the reason for this might be to do with putting your body on the line in such sports, and that to win meant that you brought your body home undamaged or less injured than your opponent. I doubt that it had anything to do with the winner being awarded a prize of bacon for his efforts, as some references suggest. It might simply have meant that he won enough money to buy food for the family and hence *Bring Home the Bacon.*

By Hook or by Crook
[determined to do something by any means possible]

I have read three or four possible derivations for this saying, but the one that stands out by far and has the most ring of truth about it is this one. In medieval times, much forest and woodland was privately owned or controlled by the monarchy as royal estates. Peasants and poor people were allowed to take deadwood from these forests (to use as fuel for fires) provided it could be pulled down with a shepherd's 'crook' or cut with a 'billhook' of the kind used when reaping crops. Hence the term *By Hook or by Crook.*

This might sound a little weak as origins go, but it is the soundest I can find by a long way and is in my view more likely than another popular suggestion. This relates to two judges, namely 'Hooke' and 'Crooke', in the seventeenth century who were renowned for solving difficult legal cases, the idea being that whatever the issue it would be solved for certain by Hooke, or by Crooke. I'm afraid I'm not convinced.

Usage of this expression today relates to the certainty of something happening, or the determination to do something without allowing anything to stop you, as in *By Hook or by Crook* I will!

Cash on the Nail
[to pay now, not later]

I lived in Bristol for many years, and shortly after moving there was taken by a friend to see some of the city. One historic attraction that he took great delight in showing me was the 'nails' in the pavement outside the old Corn Exchange, and I understand that other cities have similar features.

These 'nails' are brass tables made up of a post standing about three feet high with a flat round top perhaps two feet in diameter. This is where corn traders bought and sold grain, with deals being completed on the nails. I imagine that a price might have been quoted in two ways, perhaps 12 guineas a bushel for payment at the end of the month, or 10 guineas for immediate payment or *Cash on the Nail.*

Very much in use today, the meaning has not changed in that immediate payment is sought, although not necessarily on a pavement in Bristol.

Cat Nap
[a short sleep, a snooze]

A short sleep, most likely during the day when we are not really supposed to be sleeping, so there is some illicit feeling about the term, almost that it is a secret little snooze that has been snatched while no one is monitoring us.

As for origin, I can only suppose that it was coined because of the similarity to a cat sleeping in the day to conserve energy for a night on the prowl. I have certainly been known to *Cat Nap* but it never seems to stop me from sleeping all night as well.

Cut the Mustard
[to be of acceptable or superior standard]

The source of this saying is by no means clear. Mustard plants are quite tough and fibrous, and are difficult to cut. Also, I suppose it's true that those little mustard seeds in grainy mustard seem to resist cutting as they simply avoid the knife. It is possible that either of these gave rise to the term by meaning that it would have to be something special if it was going to *Cut the Mustard*.

Mustard is used in a number of descriptive ways: to say someone is 'absolute mustard' means he or she is exceptionally good at what they do, and the term 'as keen as mustard' is similar, although this might derive from simply meaning someone is 'hot' or 'sharp'.

Whatever the origin, the saying seems to work well in that it implies something or someone has to be above the ordinary to be able to *Cut the Mustard*.

'There was no way he could stay on the team after that poor display; he never did really *cut the mustard*.'

Doubting Thomas
[a sceptic]

As many readers will know, this has a biblical origin. Thomas was one of the twelve disciples but, unlike the others, he did not believe that Jesus had been resurrected, or that he had been seen by the eleven others, despite being told this by all of them. He continued to doubt until he had seen Jesus for himself, and had verified that it truly was the Lord by examining His crucifixion wounds.

Usually today the term is applied to anyone who refuses to believe something without being shown absolute proof.

Feet of Clay
[to have character flaws]

This saying has a clear and distinct biblical origin. The Bible tells us of a dream that Nebuchadnezzar, the King of Babylon, had in which he saw a great statue, perhaps of a god, which was for the most part made of gold, silver, and other metals, except for the feet which were partly iron and partly sludgy clay. The intended meaning was that while parts of the kingdom are strong and sturdy, some parts will be broken or weak.

The saying is used today to suggest that someone, especially a prominent person who is otherwise strong and possibly revered, has hidden weaknesses. It does not mean that someone is slow moving and resistant to change due to his or her feet being 'stuck in the mud', as I have heard it incorrectly used.

Lock, Stock, and Barrel
[everything included, the whole thing]

I have broken my rough alphabetical order here to put *Lock, Stock, and Barrel* together with two related sayings, 'flash in the pan' and to 'go off half-cocked'. These all relate to the use of an old-fashioned firearm called a musket, which was used to fight armed battles as early as the 1600s and is the forerunner of the modern rifle.

A flintlock musket consists of a barrel down which the bullet fires; a stock, which is the wooden piece that allows the musket to be held and fired from the shoulder; and the lock, which is the part that sets off the charge to fire the gun. That's it – there might be a few other additions, some decorative, some functional, but essentially the entire gun is made up of the *Lock, Stock, and Barrel*, hence the whole thing.

Flash in the Pan
[something short-lived, has not lived up to its promise]

Looking at the 'lock, stock and barrel' in a little more detail, the lock is made up of a few separate parts that together enable the gun to be fired. Gunpowder is pushed down the barrel, followed by the bullet or lead ball, and rammed firmly into the closed end at the stock by a ramrod which is usually held in a clip under the barrel so as to be ready for reloading. The pan, which is a little cup-shaped disc, and a small hole in the barrel at the lock allow a spark to ignite the gunpowder and hence fire the bullet. The spark is created by a flint striking a roughened metal plate near the pan, and to make sure ignition took place, a small amount of gunpowder is poured into the pan.

As you might imagine, this was a fairly precarious process that sometimes did not work as planned. The flint would strike and the powder in the pan would go off with a 'flash', but if the main charge of gunpowder in the barrel did not ignite, the bullet would not fire. Hence, a failure like this was just a *Flash in the Pan*.

This is used today to describe something that has not lived up to its promise or has performed less well than hoped for. The consequence for the musketeer might well have been fatal if he was then shot by an attacker due to his own weapon producing only a *Flash in the Pan*.

Go Off Half-Cocked
[to begin before ready and prepared]

The flintlock gun described above has a small lever holding the flint which is pushed hard towards the roughened metal plate by a spring, making it strike and cause a spark. This lever is on a ratchet and the action of pulling the lever back against the spring is known as cocking the weapon. There are two cocking positions, one to hold the flint free of the pan while preparing the charge, called half-cocked, and a second position using the full force of the spring, which is fully cocked. The half-cocked position is intended to be relatively safe, in that it should not have enough force to make a big enough spark to fire the gun if released by the trigger from this point.

However, guns of this kind were notoriously unreliable and it was possible for the flint to strike from the half-cocked position, either causing a 'flash in the pan' or more dangerously actually firing the bullet from the weapon – very nasty if you are not expecting it, and therefore described as *Going Off Half-Cocked*.

Modern usage means something that has happened before it was fully ready. I'm going to hold back on any humorous references to body parts, half-cocked or otherwise.

From Pillar to Post
[the whole expanse, constantly on the move from place to place]

I have seen two different fairly convincing proposed sources of this saying. The first comes from medieval punishments for minor offences, which included putting offenders in a 'pillory' that held their head and hands firmly, the deterrent being both the discomfort of this and the things thrown by passers-by, often rotten vegetables apparently, and the use of 'whipping posts' to which the miscreant was tied while being whipped. It is easy to see how 'pillory' could become 'pillar' and that, for a particular crime, the wrongdoer might be passed *From Pillar to Post* as the whole range of punishments were administered.

The second source, more likely in my opinion, is the game of Real Tennis, which is played in an indoor court not unlike squash or racquetball, unlike Lawn Tennis which is played outdoors. The Real Tennis court has pillars and posts within the playing area and, as with all of these kinds of games, it is good to keep the opponent on the run with hardly a moment to catch their breath – to have them go *From Pillar to Post* as it were.

Get Down to Brass Tacks
[concentrate on the important issues, get down to business]

Brass is a metal alloy with a lustrous appearance, which does not corrode. It has been used for centuries to make many items, including tacks although these can also be made of other metals. Brass tacks might have been considered to be one of the most basic items sold in a common hardware store and therefore to *Get Down to Brass Tacks* would be to get down to basics. Tacks in footwear to hold the sole onto a sturdy shoe or boot could be said to be getting down to the important end of things. Frankly, neither of these suggestions is convincing enough for me.

A far more likely source is that haberdashery or fabric stores would nail two brass tacks into the wooden counter-top one yard apart, making a quick and accurate way of measuring lengths of material for customers. They were probably those nice, smooth, round-topped brass tacks used in upholstery rather than carpet tacks, which might have sharp edges, or steel tacks, which would easily go rusty.

This saying is used these days to indicate a desire to put aside less important issues and get to the heart of the matter by saying, 'Let's *get down to brass tacks.*'

Grinning Like a Cheshire Cat
[smiling broadly, maybe as if to be smug about something or other]

The Cheshire Cat is of course a character in Lewis Carroll's fantasy adventure *Alice in Wonderland* and is known for its permanent very wide smile. Alice even asks why the cat grins so broadly and is given the answer that it is because he is a Cheshire Cat, and they all grin like that. However, Lewis Carroll did not invent the idea of Cheshire Cats grinning – the term was used by authors about 100 years before his works were published.

One theory I have found is that it refers to Cheshire Cheese makers, who depicted a smiling cat on the packaging of their product – a sort of 'cat who got the cheese and is happy about it' representation. That may be true, but I do wonder if it dates back to earlier than Lewis Carroll and other writers of the eighteenth and nineteenth centuries.

It might simply be that cats appear to be smug in that silky feline way as they slink about, although quite why this would be observed especially in cats from Cheshire I am at a loss to explain.

Hair of the Dog
[an alcoholic drink to cure a hangover]

A *Hair of the Dog* is a shortening of 'A hair of the dog that bit me', the 'dog' being an excess of alcohol the night before, and the 'hair' being a small snifter of the same stuff taken the morning after with the intended effect of clearing any traces of a hangover. While I am not necessarily recommending this cure, it seems that many of the more infamous 'morning after' recipes do indeed rely on alcohol for part of their magic. However, I would think it better to steer clear of the stuff for a day or so at least. Remember Jeeves administering a morning-after cure to his master Bertie Wooster? His concoction contained nothing more than raw egg, Worcester sauce, and red pepper. Hmm, on second thoughts, perhaps just abstinence is preferable, after all.

However, all that only concerns the modern usage of the saying. There is a history of dogs' hairs being used to cure bite wounds and prevent the onset of rabies, and it is most likely that the term originally derives from this activity.

Hobson's Choice
[this or nothing, take it or leave it]

I love the clarity and definite nature of this origin. Thomas Hobson was a stable owner in Cambridge in the 1500s whose business was renting out horses. He was a good liveryman and used a system of rotating his animals so that each was worked and rested in turn. Hence, a customer was not allowed to select a horse he or she liked the look of; they had to take the next one available on Hobson's schedule and were not given any other choice. So *Hobson's Choice* is not in choosing the one you like – it is taking what you are offered, or nothing at all.

In Seventh Heaven
[a state of great happiness or complete satisfaction]

Why 'seventh' I hear you ask? It seems that many religions consider heaven to exist on a number of levels or planes, and there are usually seven of these. This might be because seven is a prominent number in religious concepts: the Bible has numerous references to the number seven, the most important of which is probably God creating the heavens and the earth in six days and resting on the seventh.

Seventh Heaven is therefore the highest state of heaven that can be reached and is a portrayal of sublime happiness, which is exactly how the saying is used these days.

Kick the Bucket
[to die]

This has a simple enough meaning about which there is really no dispute – to die. But what about the origin? Once again, a number of possibilities exist along with dispute as to which is correct. I'm not going to go into all of the theories here but I will give you the one I think most likely, even though it is not a particularly nice subject.

In the past, livestock taken to slaughter were supported on a framework like a yolk which was called a 'bucket', possibly because the French word for this apparatus is a *trebuchet*. Animals in the throes of death might well flinch and *Kick the Bucket*. As I said, not a particularly pleasant subject but a saying that is certainly in common usage.

Let the Cat Out of the Bag
[to reveal something one is trying to conceal]

I have found a number of possible derivations of this phrase, but two stand out from the others. The first is linked to the 'cat of nine tails', a lash used to punish sailors who had committed some offence or other on board ship. I don't favour this proposed origin however, just because it doesn't strike me as being true.

My preference is for a more popular meaning coming from the days when piglets were taken to market to be sold. The wriggling young animal was put in a sack or bag to be carried away, and unscrupulous sellers, as you might have already guessed, sometimes replaced the pig with a cat, which had little or no value. The trick must have been to get an unsuspecting purchaser to part with his money before opening the sack, as to do so would be to *Let the Cat out of the Bag*.

The saying is commonly used today to say that a secret has been revealed.

Living on a Shoestring
[having very little means to support oneself]

There are a few different proposed origins of this, some having gambling connections, others linking shoestrings to being close to the ground and hence very low, or thin and narrow, meaning a thin budget. I suppose I could believe someone saying his finances are 'as thin as a bootlace or shoestring' so this might have some truth to it.

My preferred, although perhaps fanciful, derivation is from the days of debtors' jails where people were locked up for not paying their debts. Jails did not provide food and if you did not have a family member or friend to visit you with some provisions, you would have to pay your jailor for supplies, probably just a few crusts of bread and some water. It is said that the unfortunate inmates would beg by dangling one of their shoes by a shoestring through bars in an outside cell wall in the hope of collecting a coin or two from generous passers-by. They were thus *Living on a Shoestring*.

This was told to me by a good friend in Australia and although I like it more than most of the various possible origins I have heard, I wonder if those in jail had any shoes at all, let alone hung them through a barred cell window. Such jails might have been located in the sort of areas where this was a sure way to get your shoes stolen rather than collect charity. I'm undecided.

Mum's the Word
[to remain silent – to keep a secret]

Nothing to do with mother or her ability to keep secrets, I'm afraid. 'Mum' simply relates to making a 'mmm' sound by keeping one's lips tightly shut, perhaps also laying a finger across them to further indicate that you are not prepared to speak or reveal anything verbally.

It has become *Mum's the Word* through common usage over time.

Nineteen to the Dozen
[lively, spirited, very energetic]

It would be obvious if the saying simply meant going at the rate of nineteen while only expected to perform at a rate of twelve – of whatever is being measured. But that's not the whole story. Why nineteen, why not eighteen, or some other quantity greater than twelve?

There are various proposed explanations as to why it is nineteen and not another figure, but the one I like dates back to the use of beam engines to pump water out of mines. These machines, it is said, could pump a staggering 19,000 gallons of water for the input of just 12 bushels of coal, this being much more efficient than previous methods, and they were hence working *Nineteen to the Dozen*. Perhaps that is a little fanciful but it's the most plausible explanation I could find.

On a Sticky Wicket
[a tricky situation or predicament]

A cricketing term, obviously. Although cricket is played out-doors on grass, cricket pitches are prepared by cutting and rolling until the grass is quite short and the ground quite hard. This gives the optimum playing surface and ensures that the ball bounces correctly and in the way the bowler intends. Delivery of the ball can be pretty fierce, and batting on a good wicket can be a precarious, and potentially dangerous, affair. Wicket here does not mean the wooden stumps that the batsman is trying to protect from the bowler – it refers to the whole area around the stumps and specifically the piece of ground where the batsman is positioned. If the ground is slightly wet or has not been prepared well, the ball might not bounce as expected and might even appear to almost 'stick' to the soil, making it harder for the batsman to play a decent shot. Hence batting *On a Sticky Wicket* is less than ideal and is a situation preferably avoided.

The saying has been adopted to describe any sort of uncertain or risky condition.

Once in a Blue Moon
[a rare event, a very seldom occurrence]

The moon can sometimes appear to have a faint blue tinge which is almost always due to some form of contamination in the atmosphere, either dust from a volcanic eruption somewhere, or smoke perhaps from a forest fire. But this is definitely not the origin of the saying as it has nothing to do with the actual colour of the moon. Incidentally, after the eruption of Mount St. Helens on the west coast of the United States in 1980, from certain locations the moon appeared to be blue for many months.

The lunar cycle is 29½ days, over which time the moon goes from new to full, and then new again. There are 365 days in each year (leap year corrections excluded for the purpose of this explanation) and so there are just over 12 and one-third lunar cycles each year. As the calendar is divided into 12 months, there is approximately one lunar cycle each month, although there will be some months in which the moon is full twice in the month. As you can see from the maths this is going to happen about every third year, and it is the second full moon in a month where two full moons occur that is referred to as a blue moon, one that does not happen very often.

That's all very well, but why is this extra full moon called blue? I wonder if this comes from the word 'belie' – to belie is to be false or to be at odds with established belief. Remember that, before clocks and calendars, the moon would have been an important indicator of when to do things on a farm, for example, and moons throughout the year were named, such as the harvest moon which is in September. It could be that this second moon belied what was expected when using the sky as a calendar.

One Over the Eight
[one drink too many, to be drunk]

Although beer was definitely weaker a century or more ago when this saying probably came into existence, you might think that to have eight would be enough to get anyone drunk. In fact, beer wasn't always served in pints, or any standard measure for that matter, and to have eight glasses or more likely tankards of ale that was half the strength it is today would be the equivalent of maybe four or five pints of modern lager.

Nevertheless, that would certainly have me reeling, and one over this would definitely be a drink too many for me. The saying was probably used by hard-working and hard-drinking folk and therefore *One Over the Eight* was probably about right for a good night out on pay-day.

It is possible of course that the saying is simply a euphemism for having had too much to drink, regardless of the actual number of drinks that have been consumed, and that the figure eight is mentioned as there are eight pints in a gallon – which should be enough to get anyone well inebriated.

Peeping Tom
[one who spies on others, possibly with a sexual association]

This is said to come from the days of Lady Godiva and her naked ride on horseback through the streets of Coventry. If you aren't familiar with the tale, at some time around the year 1050, in an attempt to get her powerful husband to reduce taxes on poor townspeople, Lady Godiva performed the outrageous act of riding naked through the streets. The good people of the town agreed not to look as she rode by, but one called Tom was not going to be cheated out of a view of the naked lady and so became the first *Peeping Tom*.

In fact, although Lady Godiva and her naked exploit are documented from around that time, the story of Tom does not appear until a few centuries later, meaning that it might simply be folklore, but it is most probably the origin of the saying nevertheless.

There is a clearly a sexual overtone in the use of this saying today, as it is often used to mean observing for the purpose of one's own sexual pleasure, or to spy on others engaged in an intimate act.

Pull Out All the Stops
[to give it all you've got, to really go for it]

This one is simple enough. Church organs have what are called 'stops', buttons that are pushed in to dampen or reduce the volume, or to mute or change the sound that is made. The effect of these stops is cancelled by pulling them out and to *Pull Out All the Stops* is to play the instrument as loudly as possible.

Commonly used to mean pushing anything to its maximum output, be it a racing car or other vehicle, or just one's approach to an activity, to *Pull Out All the Stops* means to give it 100% and then some.

Red Herring
[something that distracts from an important issue]

Although there is disagreement over the origin of this saying, I think this simple notion is the most likely. Apparently, a smoked kipper is sometimes called a red herring because it turns a dark red or brown colour as part of the smoking process. It is said that once, because of its powerful smell, a kipper was dragged across fields to throw hounds off the scent of a fox – they were thereby distracted from what they should have been chasing by a *Red Herring.*

It sounds plausible enough to me. I speak from a position of some knowledge as I well remember a particular prank played on a colleague in his office, involving a cleverly hidden kipper, which as it started to smell, caused great distraction from our work. I am keen to point out that I was not responsible for this joke, however, in case by some chance he should read this book.

Save My Bacon
[to rescue or escape – perhaps from a fate such as death]

As mentioned earlier in this section, these days we think of bacon as being a specific cut of meat from a pig, but in times gone by 'bacon' was descriptive of pretty much any cut of meat from any animal, It is being used here in a slang way to mean the human body and so to *Save My Bacon* means to save me from bodily harm.

It is therefore not a request to the local butcher to put aside some nice rashers of streaky for you to collect on your way home from the office – but I am sure that possible meaning never crossed your mind.

Sewing Bee
[an organised group sewing event]

I had never understood why these are referred to as a 'bee'. There are 'spelling bees' and 'quilting bees'; there is even 'The Great British Sewing Bee', a television programme to find Britain's best amateur wielder of a needle. I had always thought it had something to do with being 'as busy as a bee', but it turns out this is not the case. Bees are very social insects and succeed by cooperating for their collective good. It is this collective action that is being referred to in naming events 'bees', hence a *Sewing Bee* is a group of people sewing, either producing a number of items or sometimes working on a single larger item by each providing her or his own piece, like a patchwork quilt, for example.

Spill the Beans
[to reveal the truth]

To *Spill the Beans* dates back to ancient Greece where council votes on some issue or other were decided by each voting member placing a coloured bean into a jar, a white bean indicating a yes vote and a black bean meaning no. To reveal the result, one of the officers spilled the beans onto a table.

You might see the similarity here with that of exclusive clubs voting whether or not to admit someone as a new member. The existing fellows would place a coloured ball into a bag, white to admit the freshman, black to deny him. The vote was therefore secret as it was not revealed who had placed which ball, but a majority of one or other colour decided his fate. This is the origin and meaning of the term to be 'blackballed' which has nothing to do with some odd initiation ceremony involving boot polish and a certain part of the male anatomy.

Stomping Ground
[familiar neighbourhood, one's home turf]

This is generally used to mean an area or vicinity with which a person is particularly familiar or in which they spend most of their time, or perhaps where they grew up or spent much of their childhood. It is sometimes stated as 'stamping ground' but either way it has the same meaning although the origin seems unclear. I and others think it is to do with the habit of bulls and other animals pounding their feet or 'stomping' on the ground either in a gesture of defiance or to signal their belief that their territory is being invaded and to warn off the intruder. Deer have been observed to do this in their rutting season, and hence the saying might be connected with sexual territorialism.

Take the Cake or Biscuit
[to be especially bad or objectionable]

This probably comes from the days when biscuits were more like small flat cakes and were baked in a similar way, so to *Take the Cake* or *Take the Biscuit* are equivalent sayings. But why would being particularly bad be described as taking the cake? At some time a cake might have been awarded as the prize for a competition or contest of some kind, and the winner literally 'took the cake' for coming first or being the best. I imagine that the saying is a sarcastic turn of speech, in that whatever is the extreme of its kind is said to take the cake or the biscuit even if this goes with it being extremely bad rather than very good.

'Well I've seen some bad goalkeeping in my time, but that certainly *takes the biscuit.*'

The Cat's Pyjamas
[best in class, superlative]

First let me dispel any thought that the 'cat' here is a domestic feline – it is not. In this context, 'cat' is a word that was used to describe flappers in the 1920s, those youngsters who broke with tradition and embraced the new styles of dance and entertainments that were emerging. Pyjamas were making an appearance as women's nightwear at about this time, mainly with the younger set, and for a while they were the latest 'must-have' day fashion item. I think you can now see how the phrase came about. It meant the latest fashionable thing, or anything which was greatly desirable.

It has become used more to describe things as being the best that can be obtained, like this book – it really is *The Cat's Pyjamas.*

There are other sayings with similar meanings that have animal associations. 'The cat's whiskers' actually refers to the normal sort of cat, and 'the bee's knees' has the same meaning although this might be an evolved form of 'the business'. As for 'the dog's b......s', enough said.

The Whole Shooting Match
[everything included]

This is similar in meaning to 'the whole ball of wax', which is of American origin, so it might be that *The Whole Shooting Match* is also from the United States but I have not been able to verify that. Nor have I been able to find a definitive source of the saying, but there are suggestions that many of the various 'the whole ...' phrases were coined by simply using some interesting-sounding words, 'the whole shebang' by way of example.

During the 1900s, shooting competitions were more common than today and it might just be that someone coined the phrase when describing such an event, or maybe even when offering his shooting gallery for sale – the targets, the gallery, the guns and ammunition, and everything associated with it – the whole shooting match, in fact!

'Oh yes, he's the manager all right. He's in charge of everything now, factory, offices, *the whole shooting match.*'

Tongue Tied
[unable to find the right words]

In fact, being tongue tied is a medical condition where the bottom of the tongue is connected to the floor of the mouth by a small piece of skin which is too far forward. If left uncorrected it would affect speech development and possibly have other side effects. Thankfully it is usually easily remedied soon after birth by a doctor simply snipping through the offending skin and releasing the tongue to perform normally.

The term has been borrowed in this saying to mean being unable to express oneself clearly or not being able to find the correct words for a given situation. It might also be used to describe the dumbfounded look and behaviour of an adolescent boy in the presence of a beautiful young girl he admires, especially when he is reduced to nervous babbling rather than coherent speech.

'You should have seen the look on Robert's face when Veronica walked into the room. He was completely *tongue tied.*'

Whipping Boy
[a stand-in to receive punishment on behalf of another]

Just as the phrase implies, when royal princes were attending school a whipping boy was substituted if the prince had done something wrong that was enough to warrant being punished, as he could not be, due to his royal standing. A pretty horrid practice I think you'll agree, except that you might be surprised to learn that, far from being just any boy chosen at random, the whipping boy was a close contemporary of the price attending the same school and the same classes. They would be close friends – the idea being that the prince would care deeply if his *Whipping Boy* were to be punished, so much so that it would deter him from wrongdoing.

Hmmm, I can't help wondering if the royal child would have been more deterred if he had received the lash himself!

White Elephant
[a liability that is not easy to dispose of]

Believe it or not, white elephants do actually exist, mostly in Thailand and Burma rather than India and Africa where there are larger populations of the muddy-grey-coloured variety. They had to have special treatment, due to the belief that they were sacred, and were therefore much more expensive to keep than an ordinary elephant, usually being owned only by royalty which added even more to their elevated status. Although they were considered to be symbols of good fortune and prosperity, they did not give any greater return for their owners, perhaps less in fact, as they would be used for show purposes rather than for work.

I think you can see the derivation of the saying now – something that is expensive to keep but gives less value than it is worth. The meaning of the saying is unchanged today; a *White Elephant* is something that has cost more than it ought to or requires more upkeep than a similar item, and is more trouble than it is worth.

PART 5
Obvious? Perhaps Not

It has to be said, I suppose, that the origins of most of the sayings in this section are fairly obvious, or at least that the obvious derivation turns out to be the true one. There are some intriguing ideas, however, such as a number of sayings thought to have come from the fear of being mistakenly buried alive, or why the 'dog days of summer' are so called. And who would have thought that there really was an Uncle Robert in 'Bob's your uncle'? I invite you to read on.

All Above Board
[honest and open – nothing concealed]

You might well think as I did that this is a nautical saying and that above board means above the deck, in other words in full view and not hidden below decks or down in the ship's hold. I have found suggestions that this is the origin and even that it relates to pirates hiding below decks in order to get their ship alongside the vessel they intended to board and plunder. Attractive though this image is, I think it more likely that the true origin of the saying comes from gambling and the days when card games were regularly played in London clubs and American saloons. Playing with one's hands above the table was to be playing fairly with no chance of switching or marking cards, and was said to be *All Above Board*.

It would seem there is a strong link between this and 'under hand' which presumably means the opposite of above board. The saying 'cards on the table' is also a reference to revealing the truth, or to be open and truthful over something.

An Arm and a Leg
[a large amount of money – something which is very costly]

One suggestion for this, but a fairly grisly one, is that it refers to the price paid by soldiers who lose limbs in war. So for a battle to have cost an arm and a leg would be a very high price indeed. Not a very nice thought at all. The origin might be simply that paying a large amount of money just feels as if one is giving up a limb or two, in the same way as people say, 'I'd give my right arm for one of those new gizmos.'

However, another proposed derivation strikes a chord with me. Apparently, long before the days of photography, when portraits were commissioned it clearly took longer for the artist to paint the whole person seated or standing, rather than just the head and shoulders, and the price for this was so much more that it was referred to as costing *An Arm and a Leg*, as these parts of the body were included in the picture.

Bare-Faced Lie
[a blatant untruth – an unconcealed lie]

The hidden meaning in this saying is that the lie is unconcealed – no attempt is made to cover it up or to weave it into some possible half-truth or white lie. The origin is a belief that it is much more difficult to pretend not to be lying with a clean-shaven face than with a beard or something covering the face, as facial expressions give so much away.

Those who study body language say that many people subconsciously put their hand to their face when telling a lie, or look away from the person they are speaking to, presumably to stop themselves from revealing the lie. But the action of raising their hand in this way can be interpreted as covering up a lie, so that the untruth is revealed anyway.

Barking Up the Wrong Tree
[a mistaken assumption]

This is an easy one and the obvious is in fact the true origin. It refers to hunting dogs who having chased a less fortunate creature that has escaped and is hiding up a tree, stand at the bottom and bark, often front paws raised on the trunk and looking skywards in the mistaken belief that their quarry is above them, when in fact it is up another tree altogether.

This is generally used to describe almost any situation where a mistaken assumption is made.

Beat Around the Bush
[to avoid discussing something embarrassing or awkward]

This really does mean what it says. Beaters are used in shooting to rouse the birds from the ground into the air, in order for them to be picked off by a host of shooters with shotguns. But even before this kind of shoot, birds were hunted by trapping them in nets without them getting into flight, and the bushes they were in would be beaten to make them emerge from the undergrowth. Beating around the bush was done to get the birds to cluster in one place, and then the bush itself would be beaten to get them to emerge and be caught. So to *Beat Around the Bush* was to build up to the act of catching the prey, but was not the main event.

Often used today to mean prevarication or avoidance of the main point, this saying still has effectively the same meaning.

'Come on, stop **beating around the bush**. Just tell us. Did you get the job or didn't you?'

Bitter Pill
[something unpleasant that must be accepted]

Before the days of large multinational pharmaceutical companies, the business of making drugs into pills was much less sophisticated and sugary coatings had not yet been thought of.

A doctor would sometimes even mix powdered ingredients and press them into pills himself, making them easier for the patient to swallow. But the taste of the ingredients was unmasked and many of these had a very nasty taste – quinine, for example, which was used to treat malaria is incredibly bitter. And so the term came about. The pill might be bitter or unpalatable; nevertheless, it has to be taken if you are to be cured.

The saying is used today to describe a situation where the truth is difficult to accept.

Bob's Your Uncle
[everything will be all right]

I love the origin I have found for this saying and I so hope it is true. It just typifies the way in which I have always that thought people in powerful positions abuse their authority, especially in days gone by when it was less likely to be found out.

In the late 1800s the prime minister of the day, Lord Salisbury whose name was Robert Gascoyne-Cecil, appointed his favoured nephew Arthur Balfour to various important political posts that he might not have achieved had it not been for the family connection. Thus, it is said, he reached these positions purely because Robert was his uncle. Balfour himself went on to become prime minister and the working classes coined the phrase *Bob's Your Uncle* to mean 'Don't worry, everything will be all right' or 'Everything will be taken care of for you'.

Busman's Holiday
[a holiday or break on which one does similar activities to one's usual work]

Presumably a busman's holiday is so called because it was usual some decades ago for people to travel to their holiday destination by bus, especially if this was one of the popular English coastal resorts, Blackpool or Skegness, for example. If your day job was working on the buses, the idea is that it was not much of a holiday to travel by bus.

The saying has wider application of course; taking a few days off to do some jobs around the house is a busman's holiday if you work as a builder or maintenance man. Expecting one's wife to do household chores at a holiday apartment you own is most definitely a busman's holiday for her, especially if she does all of the housework at home.

The saying is also used where no actual holiday is involved, if you are driving the kids around all weekend, for example and you work as a taxi-driver, or cooking for the family when you work in a kitchen. All of these can be said to be a *Busman's Holiday*.

Butter Someone Up
[to flatter, perhaps exaggeratedly so]

It is pretty clear that this is usually used to describe being unusually nice or flattering to a person in the hope of favourable treatment in return. But why do we say to *Butter Someone Up*? I believe it is a simple as the act of buttering a slice of bread or toast. Plain bread is itself rather dull, but with some delicious tasting butter it is much more appealing, especially if the butter is laid on thickly.

Another source tells us that in India, clarified butter is thrown at statues of their gods, and in Chinese culture, butter sculptures would bring good fortune for the upcoming year. That may be, but I am not convinced that either of these is the source of the saying.

Can't See the Wood for the Trees
[focusing on details and missing the main point]

There may be some confusion here, in that 'wood' does not mean the material a tree consists of, but wood as in 'forest' – it might be better written as 'Can't see the forest for the trees'. The meaning is clear, however – seeing only the details (individual trees), rather than the entire wood or forest (the big picture). Missing the entirety of a situation due to seeing only small details is what is happening when we *Can't See the Wood for the Trees.*

Champagne Socialist
[one espousing socialism while living an extravagant lifestyle]

There are plenty of these aren't there? Politicians who talk-the-talk of the working classes in order to pretend to be of-the-people and have the interests of the poorer in society at heart, while sending their own children to expensive public schools, enjoying private health care and other benefits, and living in an extravagant manner perhaps even at public cost. Their rivals are quick to point out these inconsistencies, but of course the same is almost certainly happening on both sides of the political divide. That's not to say that a great many politicians do not care deeply about the welfare of society at large and not all of them are hypocritical to the extent I have depicted.

Chink in the Armour
[a minor weakness but one which might cause severe problems]

I do not know if this actually originates from the time when armour was worn to go into battle but that is clearly the figurative meaning of the saying. A weakness or gap in the covering of the armour is the 'chink', an opening or narrow gap, and this weakness would be the point on which an attacker would focus his sword or dagger. So, in that circumstance, a *Chink in the Armour* could be very serious indeed, possibly fatal.

Chip on One's Shoulder
[to bear a grudge, to be angry or have a grievance]

It is a matter of record from the mid-1700s that workers in naval dockyards building wooden ships were allowed to take home off-cuts of timber and that these 'chips' of wood, some being quite substantial in size, were carried on their shoulders. It was decided that this practice was becoming too costly for the yards and, to limit the amount workers could take, they were to carry the material only under their arm. This was unpopular and the workers rebelled by refusing to take their chips under their arms but keeping them on their shoulders. They were prepared to fight for their rights.

The shipyards won the day eventually and timber could no

longer be removed on workers' shoulders, but the saying stuck
– someone with a grievance was said to have a *Chip on His
Shoulder.*

It is also said that, in some cultures, young men to show
their worth will place a chip of wood on one of their shoulders
and invite others to knock it off, by which action they issued
a challenge to a fight. Either way, the phrase clearly means
someone with a grudge or a grievance, or spoiling for a fight.

Coals to Newcastle
[a pointless exercise]

What the reader needs to know here is that the Newcastle area
was traditionally the biggest producer of coal in Britain and
that the local economy was almost entirely dependent on coal
at one time. So to take *Coals to Newcastle* or to try to sell coal
to the area would be a completely foolhardy venture.

Taking sand to the desert is a similar phrase you might have
heard, with the same meaning.

Daylight Robbery
[grossly overcharging]

Not all robberies take place at night where the thief has the
partial protection of darkness; some happen in broad daylight.
In fact I witnessed one in a jewellery store on a bright Saturday
afternoon in the high street. That particular event displayed
some bare-faced cheek for sure, but it was not daylight robbery
in the meaning of this phrase.

What is being referred to here is not actual robbery at all, but the act of being exorbitantly overcharged for something, perhaps because the seller has the power to do so because of the situation – selling umbrellas in the rain for example. Being charged much more than the normal price in such circumstances could be described as *Daylight Robbery*.

It is said by some that the phrase originates from the late 1600s when window taxes were first levied in England as a way of raising treasury funds. This is why there are many examples of bricked-up windows in buildings of this age, as owners avoided paying the hated window tax. The authorities taking away daylight in this way might be thought to be the source of the phrase daylight robbery, but apparently the saying was not recorded until two centuries afterwards and therefore the link is not so strong as to be certain.

Dead Ringer
[an exact likeness]

A *Dead Ringer* is not someone who once rang the bells at the local church but has since died. Seriously, a 'ringer' is a substitute or duplicate of something or other, originally apparently a horse which was substituted for another in order to either win or lose a race as opposed to what was expected from the original animal. Clearly this was with fraudulent intent, either to fool the bookmakers into giving the wrong odds, or the punters into betting on a horse with no hope. The word 'dead' simply means 'dead on' or accurate, in that an exact likeness would be required for the deceit to work.

I have heard that the word 'ringer' is used in the second-hand car trade, where unscrupulous dealers substitute either a vehicle or its registration for another to give a false but favourable history to a car that does not deserve it, or even to cover up the fact that a car has previously been completely wrecked.

It is also, of course, used to describe a person's 'double', as in 'He's a dead ringer for George Clooney,' meaning that the likeness is so clear that the ringer is often mistaken for the famous actor himself. Doubles making supposed celebrity appearances at events can earn a good living it seems.

Dog Days of Summer
[hot, dry, lazy period in July and August]

We all love those long, hot, dry summer days, don't we? Or at least most of us do. But why are they called the 'dog days'? I thought it might be something to do with it being so hot that dogs – who cannot sweat through their skin to cool down and have to rely on sweating from their tongue, which is why they pant when they are hot – just laze around looking exhausted at this time of year. However, and not for the first time, it turns out that my theory is completely wrong.

The 'dog' being referred to is the Dog Star, or Sirius to give it its proper name, and observers in Mediterranean countries noted its conjunction (rising and setting at the same time) with the Sun to be in the period from early July through to about mid-August, and that this coincided with the hottest part of the year, hence the dog days of summer.

It is also noteworthy that these early observers were not concerned with this time of year being best for holidaymakers, as such activities did not exist in these times. They associated it with being uncomfortably hot and prone to the spread of disease, an unpleasant period, whereas we probably think of the *Dog Days of Summer* as being an agreeable time if perhaps a little hotter than ideal.

The actual dates on which Sirius's conjunction takes place will be different depending on the position on Earth from which it is viewed, and that is why the origin of the saying was specific to Mediterranean observers. The dates will have changed over time anyway due to something called planetary precession, and of course they only apply in the northern hemisphere as July and August are winter months in the southern hemisphere.

Dream Ticket
[a perfect combination or pairing]

Nearly always used to describe a pairing of two political candidates who individually appeal to different sections of the public and who will poll more votes together than on their own. A presidential and vice-presidential candidate duo for example, where each holds slightly differing views but both are on the same side of the main political divide, will attract interest from a wider audience, and hence be difficult for opponents to win against. In fact, John F. Kennedy and Lyndon B. Johnson were the first dream ticket in 1961, but the name has been applied to many other pairs since.

   I have heard the saying used in a non-political context. A particular duo of Manchester United football strikers in the 1990s were referred to in this way, and more recently a pairing in the Ryder Cup golf competition were so complimentary in their style and success as to be called a *Dream Ticket*.

Dyed in the Wool
[resistant to change – perhaps with strong opinions]

Please note: this is dyed, not died. The meaning comes from dyeing wool, a practice that goes back many years, since it was discovered long ago that wool could be cut from sheep and turned into fabric and garments. Dyes are made from naturally occurring substances and are permanent, otherwise colours would simply wash out or fade very quickly. So the action of dyeing wool was permanent – once the colour was put in, it couldn't be taken out or changed. That is the derivation of the saying, something which cannot be changed.

Today, we often use the phrase to mean someone with strong opinions that they are unlikely ever to change regardless of what might happen.

Graveyard Shift
[working late or through the night]

There are a lot of theories that this saying has to do with someone given the job of watching over a grave at night after a burial that day, to ensure that the person interred has not been buried alive, although it seems most of these possible meanings have been discredited as incorrect.

I am fairly sure that the origin is simply being at work or having the shift which starts around midnight. This is, after all, called the 'witching hour' and might well be associated with graveyards. Also, sailors called the midnight to four o'clock watch the 'graveyard watch', probably because this was potentially the most dangerous time of night and the watch on which most perilous things tended to occur.

Another common usage I have noted is when attending conferences or seminars – speakers refer to the slot immediately after lunch as the *Graveyard Shift*, probably either because only half the audience have made it back in time and the meeting room resembles a graveyard – lots of chair backs but no people – or because those who are in attendance are sleepy and might as well be dead for all the attention they are giving the orator.

Hat Trick
[scoring three successive goals or points in a sporting contest]

It is a simple enough definition and one with which all football spectators will be familiar, but in fact the term has a cricketing origin. It is recorded that, in 1858, a certain H.H. Stevenson took three wickets with three consecutive balls, a feat which presumably had not been achieved before or at least not recorded, as on this occasion a collection was held and a hat was purchased and presented to him. The practice of scoring three times in a single match in various sports has since been known as a *Hat Trick*.

I wonder what would have happened if he had been presented with some other item of clothing, or any object for that matter, instead of a hat. A 'trouser trick' might give the wrong impression altogether, and a 'two crystal tumblers and a decanter trick' just isn't as catchy, is it?

Have Itchy Feet
[a desire to travel or move – a desire to make a change]

This is truly idiomatic, in that the literal meaning is far from the intended meaning of the saying. Itchy feet can be cured I'm sure, or at least be treated by any of a number of foot powders or ointments available from the chemists.

To have itchy feet in the sense of the saying means to have a desire to move or to travel. I have a friend who, in the words of his wife, is 'either on a trip or planning the next one'. He clearly has itchy feet and is an inveterate traveller, and will be until he 'gets cold feet' so to say.

I heard this phrase used recently to describe someone's desire to change jobs. Having got tired of her current role and wanting to move on, she was said to *Have Itchy Feet*, a different and more modern usage.

In the Pink
[to be in good health]

I have heard, as you might have, that this saying derives from those jolly chaps and gals who enjoy foxhunting, or riding to hounds as I believe it is called. Standard clothing for this activity is a scarlet jacket among other items, and one famous maker of the jackets is a certain Thomas Pink. Hence if you were happy in the saddle chasing over fields after a small furry animal, you were said to be *In the Pink*.

I have to say I was always a little sceptical over this origin although it might have some truth. I have since found out that there is a record of the saying being used before Mr Pink started making the famous red jackets. I'm not sure that any of the other possible derivations has any more claim to being the true origin, however, but I like the idea of it being linked to 'pinking' which is the action of cutting or trimming a neat edge on something and is why pinking shears are so called. The theory goes that something that has been neatly cut or trimmed is said to have been pinked or in the pink. Not totally convincing, is it?

I offer a final possibility, that ruddy cheeks have been considered a sign of good health through the ages and that being *In the Pink* simply refers to a glow on one's face. I don't know of course whether ruddy cheeks really are a sign of good health. Perhaps they are the opposite, especially if they are caused by an over-indulgence in wine, but it might be the correct source of the saying, nevertheless.

In the Same Boat
[sharing the same problem]

I like this origin because it truly encapsulates the meaning of the saying for me. It comes from times when boats were used for transport far more than they are today, and when sometimes quite small boats would be used to convey large numbers of people. This could be a perilous activity, especially if weather conditions were not good and the potential risks involved were shared by all of those undertaking the voyage.

The fate of each one of them was inextricably linked with all the others and they were quite literally all *In the Same Boat*.

Long in the Tooth
[old, an old person]

Animals' teeth are to some extent an indication of the health of the beast, but can also reveal their age due to size and wear. Horse traders are known to look at the teeth of their stock and can determine age fairly closely by this, I am told. The animals' teeth continue to grow through their life so, apart from wear or breakage, length of teeth can again be used to determine age, hence *Long in the Tooth* meaning old.

The saying is really applied to humans, however, and to be a bit long in the tooth for something is to imply that one is perhaps a little too old for some activity or other these days.

Not Over Until the Fat Lady Sings
[don't assume the outcome is known or certain]

The 'fat lady' just has to be an operatic reference, either to a particular character in some opera or other, or to a performer. I like the notion that it is Brünnhilde in Wagner's famous Ring Cycle. This is made up of four separate operas, the whole thing lasting around 15 hours when performed as the composer intended, and Brünnhilde, often a substantial soprano, does indeed sing at the end of the fourth part. The whole thing is not staged as one single performance, it is done in four separate shows; nevertheless each is quite a lengthy operation and it might not be clear to the audience when the epic is due to end. If they know the story, they will also know that until Brünnhilde begins her final aria, it will not be over – until the fat lady sings.

I can well imagine one audience member asking a neighbour does he or she know when it will be over, and the reply being, 'Not until the fat lady sings!'

I apologise now if I have offended anyone with this use of 'fat lady'.

Off the Hook
[freed from a commitment or task]

It is not easy to find a definitive source for this phrase but I think it is a fishing term. To be on the hook is clearly to be caught and being reeled in by the angler, so to be off the hook or to be 'let off the hook' must be to have escaped the unpleasantness of being captured.

References to meat being on hooks in slaughterhouses and butcheries, and it being a relief to be *Off the Hook*, are also a possible origin but I think the fishing basis is more likely.

Over the Hill
[old, perhaps too old for the matter at hand]

The 'hill' in question is one's life and the mid-point is the top of the hill. So in early years, and before the halfway stage, we are still climbing the hill, but to be over the hill implies being beyond the middle of one's years and on the downward stretch towards the end.

Oh the foolishness of youngsters today! Don't they realise that all the fun is being had by those of us who are well *Over the Hill* already!

Piece of Cake
[something easy to accomplish – not a problem]

This is similar in every way to 'as easy as pie', which is probably American in origin, whereas cake is most likely the English version. It is used to mean a task which is a pleasure to fulfil rather than a chore. I well remember my daughter when she was quite young being asked to help in the kitchen with some errand or other answering, 'Sure Dad, piece of cake.'

Quite why we would say this when meaning something simple is somewhat of a mystery to me. Making cake is simple enough I suppose, although it has its technicalities and to make a really good one requires a certain skill. It is thought that the origin dates back to when cakes were given as prizes in competitions and the winner would say their triumph was easily achieved, a *Piece of Cake* in fact.

Pig in a Poke
[not what you thought it to be – not the genuine article]

As already described in 'Let the Cat out of the Bag' earlier in this book, the saying comes from the practice of selling piglets at market, and transporting them there in a sack, this being the 'poke' from the French word for bag which is *poque*. It was very advisable to see the contents of the bag before buying, as unscrupulous sellers substituted an inferior animal, typically a cat for the pig – and your *Pig in a Poke* turned out not to be a pig after all, and so not the genuine article.

Pop Your Clogs
[to die]

No dispute here as to the meaning of the phrase, it is definitely a euphemism for dying, but why clogs and what does 'Pop' mean? One possible explanation is that working class people in some industries wore clogs and although these were necessary while living, they were no longer needed when a person died. The clogs might therefore be pawned or sold, either to raise much-needed cash for the family or perhaps to help pay for funeral costs. It is believed that the word 'Pop' in this context was at some time in the past common usage for 'to pawn', and if so this makes sense of the saying to *Pop Your Clogs*.

Saved by the Bell
[rescued at the last minute]

This is another saying with theories that it originates from being buried alive, and that some apparatus with a string and a bell was attached to corpses in coffins so that they could signal not being dead and therefore be saved by the bell. As with other similar phrases, this possible origin has been disproved and never sounded correct to me.

It is clear I think that the true source is from the sport of boxing. Boxing matches are divided into a number of rounds of a few minutes each, with a break of one minute or so between them, the end of each round being signalled by the time keeper ringing a bell. If a fighter is knocked down during a round, he must recover to his feet in a fit state to continue the match within ten seconds, the count being given by the referee. If he does not recover within this time, he has been 'knocked out' and his opponent is declared the winner immediately. However, if the end of the round occurs before the ten seconds are up, he has longer to recover and is allowed to fight on at the start of the next round.

He has quite literally therefore been *Saved by the Bell.*

Stuffed Shirt
[very formal – or to behave in a formal manner]

Dictionaries describe this as a 'derogatory term' applied to someone who is overly formal or acting in an old fashioned perhaps even a pompous manner. Well, I've been called some derogatory terms in my life but *Stuffed Shirt* has got to be the softest form of derogation I've heard. Seriously though, I find it a rather neat and tidy way of saying that someone is acting as if they are more important than they are, possibly by puffing out their chest in pride, giving the impression that their shirt is stuffed with something or other, although it is not much used these days.

[Like] The Black Hole of Calcutta
[something extremely dark or black]

When describing some dark or dingy spot my father was often heard to say, 'It's like the *Black Hole of Calcutta* down there.' Although I never asked him, I hope he hadn't visited the actual place as it was apparently a dungeon in Calcutta where many British prisoners were held by Bengali troops in 1756. Conditions were so bad that it is claimed (although not confirmed) that of 146 prisoners captured, 123 died in a single night. There are other such stories of encounters and battles with grim consequences as India fought to maintain its independence around this time.

Under the Weather
[ill – feeling out of sorts]

Why would we say under the weather when feeling unwell? I believe this comes from the days when voyages were made on ocean liners rather than aircraft as they are today. Bad weather at sea caused ships to rock and sway, often producing extreme seasickness among the passengers. The weather system responsible would be above the immediate area the vessel was sailing in and hence the ship was *Under the Weather*, the saying becoming applied to those feeling the effects of this.

Conversely I suppose an aeroplane in flight might be said to be 'above the weather' although I have been on some rough flights in my time and can confirm that air travel is not immune from making passengers feel pretty awful sometimes.

Another note regarding this saying: I did not include it in Part 2, Of Nautical Origin, as it was not used by sailors and naval crews but by travellers on passenger liners, which I consider to be a different classification if you will.

Water Under the Bridge
[something which has happened and cannot now be altered – events in the past]

I cannot find much reference to the usage of this saying, nor to the origin, except that it appeared in print as early as the 1800s. It is clear that it means something which has passed or happened in the past, but I suppose the wider meaning is that it cannot be undone or changed. There is a feeling when using the phrase that it refers to water flowing only in one direction, but this would not be true in the case of a tidal river such as the Thames, and London has been the source of many of these kinds of sayings.

So we must be content with the simplest of definitions, that *Water Under the Bridge* is something which has passed and cannot be gone back over.

PART 6
Often Mispronounced

We should probably not laugh at mistakes made when using the following sayings, as scope for mispronunciation and misunderstanding is possibly greater in the English language than any other. I am reminded of the schoolboy joke that goes like this: a person says to his friend, 'Have you got that six quid you owe me?' only to be repaid by his friend with a 'sick squid', the debt being settled as far as the friend is concerned. It wasn't that funny all those years ago either, but you see what I mean. The few sayings collected here are almost always either misspoken or misspelt, and you can see why.

A Damp Squib
[something that does not reach the expected level of excitement]

You've heard this pronounced incorrectly I'm sure – a 'damp squid' is what I remember hearing. Of course a squid would be damp, they live in water, don't they, actually underneath it I think!

A squib is in fact a firework or firecracker, a banger as they were colloquially known when I was at school. And a damp one does not go bang – it gives more a fizz or a muffled *phut*. This saying is used today to describe anything which fails to reach the anticipated level, whether through getting wet or not.

A Hare-Brained Scheme
[a crazy or wild and foolish idea, possibly something unlikely to succeed]

The correct spelling is indeed 'hare' but apparently it has been spelt 'hair' in the past, so perhaps either spelling is acceptable. Most dictionaries have the correct spelling as one word, 'hare-brained', with definitions ranging from 'silly' to 'impractical'.

Some sources suggest the origin as being that one's brain has no more substance than a hair, but I think a more likely heritage is the linkage with 'as mad as a March hare', implying that the scheme in question is no more sensible than a March hare and just plain crazy.

'Oh no, not another one of Uncle Harry's **hare-brained schemes**,' said Auntie Jean as a she saw him hurtle past the window in a soapbox on wheels.

A Mine of Information
[a person or reference source with a large amount of information]

That's a 'mine' not a 'mind' of information, although in this case the mispronounced version works almost as well as the original. It is intended quite simply to describe the information source as deep and extensive – as in a vast mine which has been cut deep into the ground, stretching out far and in many directions. I only wish that someone would attach the term to me.

Beyond the Pale
[beyond toleration or acceptability]

Another easily misspelt saying – it is 'pale' not 'pail'. Pale is from the same source as palisade; a pale is one of the stakes used to make up a fence when placed in a line with the bottom end pushed into the ground. The pale can refer to the piece of land enclosed by the fence or may simply refer to the line of the fence itself. Whichever, to go *Beyond the Pale* is to be outside the safe or known area, or to be outside a boundary or jurisdiction. So the saying today means just that, to go beyond acceptable limits or outside one's authority.

It always amuses me whenever I see this written incorrectly as 'beyond the pail'. What can the writer possibly think it means? Perhaps they imagine that it involves a bucket of water or something similar.

Hue and Cry
[a loud and perhaps angry statement of disapproval]

This is not so much mispronounced as misspelt, the 'hue' being often written as 'hew' or some other variant, possibly because hue is associated with colours and it is therefore assumed that this spelling cannot be correct in this context. But in fact hue comes from an old French word '*huer*' meaning to shout, and cry I suppose comes simply from outcry. It is used today to describe a noisy expression of anger, more likely to be from a group than an individual, such as a public outcry. No linkage of course with the popular singing duo 'Hue and Cry' made up of brothers Pat and Greg Kane from Manchester.

No Holds Barred
[without restrictions, everything permitted]

Often mispronounced as 'no holes barred', this is correctly stated as *No Holds Barred*, the holds being wrestling holds. There are many forms of wrestling and it is a regulated sport (at least it is these days) in which some moves and holds are against the rules. A completely free form of the sport is referred to as no holds barred, meaning that any hold is permitted, and none is disallowed. It might have been used to describe a prize-fight or back-street bout organised for illicit gain. Today it has been adopted generally to mean anything goes.

Off Your Own Bat

[as a result of your own actions, accredited to you]

This saying falls firmly into this Often Mispronounced section, as it is frequently but incorrectly said to be 'off your own back'.

Again, more than one possible origin can be found, but the one I prefer and believe to be the most likely is from the game of cricket in which scoring is tallied by counting 'runs'. After a batsman hits the ball he (or perhaps she these days, as England's female cricket team recently gave Australia a good thrashing) has the opportunity to score runs, either by running between the ends of the pitch or without having to physically run if the ball is hit to the boundary of the ground. 'Extra' runs are also counted for other reasons, if the ball is bowled wider than permitted for example, and for other errors not attributable to the batsman. These are not due to his or her skill with the bat, whereas those scored by striking the ball are off his or her own bat, as they result directly from the batsman's actions.

When comparing batsmen's abilities, it is of course sensible to consider only those runs scored off their own bats.

One Fell Swoop
[a decisive and merciless action]

This is clearly recorded in history (and used by Shakespeare) as *One Fell Swoop*, not as I have often heard it mispronounced, 'one fowl swoop'. When I learned that it derives from a bird of prey swooping fiercely to kill and take whatever poor creature it has been hovering over, I assumed the 'fell' was a hillside or other landscape feature. However, I am reliably informed that the word fell is from the same source as 'felon', in other words a cold-blooded or heartless person. So the fell swoop is a cold-blooded and merciless act.

On Tenterhooks
[awaiting news restlessly]

Nothing to do with tents I'm afraid, but that's not where the mispronunciation occurs – the mistake is to say 'tenderhooks' rather than 'tenterhooks'. The word refers to cloth being stretched out to dry, perhaps as part of an age-old manufacturing process. The hooks were used to secure the cloth onto a frame, which was known as a 'tenter', hence tenterhooks. It has become used to mean that one's nerves are stretched in anxiety over some impending information or news.

Perhaps 'tenderhooks' is appropriate after all, as the person waiting might well benefit from some tender treatment. But still it is nothing to do with tents; a person who sleeps under canvas is a camper, not a tenter.

Those poor kids were ***on tenterhooks*** all morning waiting for their exam results to come through.

Printed and Website References

These books and websites were of great help in researching the origins and meanings of various sayings and expressions. I offer many thanks to all of them.

The Penguin Dictionary of English Idioms – 2nd Edition, Daphne M Gulland and David Hinds-Howell
(Penguin Books, 2002)

The Concise Oxford English Dictionary – Main Edition
(Oxford Dictionaries, 2011)

Webster's American English Dictionary
(Merriam-Webster Inc., 2011)

https://answers.yahoo.com
http://www.collinsdictionary.com
http://dictionary.cambridge.org
http://english.stackexchange.com
http://en.wikipedia.org/wiki/Idiom
http://www.factmonster.com
http://idioms.thefreedictionary.com
http://www.joe-ks.com
http://www.knowyourphrase.com
http://www.oxforddictionaries.com
http://www.phrases.org.uk
http://www.wisegeek.com
http://www.word-detective.com

.